E is for EATING:

AN ALPHABET OF GREED

E is for EATING:
AN ALPHABET OF GREED

Tom Parker Bowles

with drawings by Matthew Rice

LONG BARN BOOKS

PUBLISHED BY
LONG BARN BOOKS

Ebrington Gloucestershire GL55 6 NW

First Published 2004

Copyright © Tom Parker Bowles 2004

Set in New Century Schoolbook.

Printed in China.

ISBN 1-902421-10-8

Contents

For BOPPA

A for ALFRESCO

So we get the chance to eat al fresco once or twice a year. And when the fates smile down on us (via a cloudless sky and balmy sun), there is no better way to dine. A plump, sweet sausage between your fingers, the grass beneath your feet and the gentle glug of a bottle of crisp white wine. Al fresco is a typically bucolic Italian phrase, more suited to the sun-dried hills of Tuscany than the rain-braised moors of North Yorkshire. But the tradition, in this country anyway, sprang from medieval hunting feasts of the 14th Century, where a hearty meal of pastries, hams and other baked meats would provide sustenance before the thrill of the chase. Sadly, not every al fresco experience turns out to be a merry event. We've all experienced those hellish outdoor washouts – the grey-skied, drizzling excuse for a fine day that English summer does so well. The white wine is lukewarm, the Thai green curry that seemed such a good idea at the time has leaked all over the strawberries, and your River Café chocolate cake has melted across the back seat, freshly regurgitated by a sorry looking dog. Munching miserably on a processed Scotch Egg, the promised vision of Albion in all her rustic glory has been replaced by a less prosaic view of the inside of the windscreen. The only wasp brave enough to face the summer storms has managed to find your face, and the ants seem undeterred by the damp grass. Disconsolate, depressed and filled with ill will, you vow that next time you'll cut out the fuss and munch a Prêt A Manger sandwich in the comfort of your own drive.

But on those rare, Wordsworthian days when man and nature reach their perfect harmony, there is nothing that can beat the sheer joy of a proper picnic. Forget Rolls Royces, silver service and butlers hired by the hour. Location and good friends are as important as the food itself. Willow trees provide elegant shade, a large rug is all that's needed for comfort and a whole array of fresh, simple food for fingers: freshly boiled shrimp with a pungent aioli; tomatoes still warm from the sun; a filling hunk of eggy tortilla; soft boiled organic eggs with a pile of celery salt; the company of close friends and copious amounts of flinty Chablis; fat-flecked salamis; slices of sweet prosciutto, sliced as thin as tissue paper; smoke infused (not flavoured) smoked salmon, the good stuff without a hint of grease; and a couple of golden baguettes. The pièce de résistance is that blissful hour between day and dusk, when the colours start to soften and blur into a haze. The distant sound of church bells accompanies the gurgle and spit of the nearby stream, and the soft hum of insects becomes a soothing balm, rather than a shrill irritation. As darkness falls, you lie down, cushioned by the feeling that all is well in the world.

Apple

We now have over two thousand species of apple in Britain. But how many of these do we actually eat? About four. Granny Smith, Golden Delicious, Cox's Orange Pippin and Royal Gala – with Bramley Seedling for cooking – dominate the supermarkets, not because of their flavour, but because they promise uniform size, shape and texture. Although they travel well and look good, they don't excite the taste buds much. What about the splendidly monikered Pig's Nose Pippin, Winter Banana, Scotch Dumpling and Poor Man's Profit, all with markedly different flavours and character? How many of these have you even heard of let alone eaten? We are happy to ignore a huge chunk of our culinary heritage in favour of pre-packaged, granite-hard pieces of tasteless pap.

B for BACON

I'm a bacon perfectionist; it has to be smoked, and must be organic or free-range. Just at that fleeting moment when the crisp, golden fat starts to take on the merest hint of caramel brown, it's time to take it out of the pan. Underdone, and I find myself transported back to the splinter-filled school breakfast bench, poking at a sorry scrap of foam flecked flesh, pinker than a Barbara Cartland blusher. Overdone, and it becomes little more than crunchy charcoal (though my uncle, for example, wouldn't have it any other way).

We're a nation with some of the finest porkers in the world; the grand Gloucester Black Spot, the mighty Tamworth, the saintly Middle Spot. Yet when it comes to choosing our rashers, what do we usually go for? Yup, slimy old imported Danish special. The majority of cheap bacon is injected with polyphosphates, which absorb and retain water, and so add watery weight to the product. When it hits the frying pan this short cut is rumbled; all you are left with is a spitting sea of white, smelly scum and a tasteless curled up scrap of meat. And that's not all. The pig, as he's so resilient, is one of the most abused animals in intensive farming. Many (though not all) industrially raised pigs are reared indoors on concrete, with hardly enough room to fart let alone root around and snuffle sweetly. The cocktail of feeds which they're forced to gulp down is often made up of an unappetizing blend of chemicals and high protein feeds, which aims to get the pig ready for market in the shortest possible time, and with the least possible amount of fat. Flavour and animal welfare come a poor second to profit margins and speed of growth. But responsible farmers, both free range and organic, treat these intelligent beasts with the respect and care that they deserve. The finest bacon comes from pigs that are kept outside, with plenty of space to scratch and rootle, and a warm, straw-packed shelter freely available to them. The meat is allowed to develop slowly, their diet is varied and interesting, and life is lived as nature intended. I usually buy organic, but there are plenty of non-organic farmers who produce some seriously good bacon to equally high standards. The problem with the rare and pure breed pigs is that they take so long to come on (and are therefore more expensive to rear, and buy). The end result is bacon to die for and this hard work pays dividends in the final product; rich, salty and deeply flavoursome, it adds porky pungency to any dish.

As for smoked over plain – my taste is for smoked, though there are some pretty lip smacking, unsmoked varieties out there. But all dry cured bacons are made in the same fashion. A mixture of salt, saltpetre (which preserves the colour of the meat) and a little brown sugar is rubbed into the belly. This is then left for twenty four hours in a cool place, then the leached salty liquid is poured off; the process is repeated daily for up to two weeks. If you want smoked, let the bellies dry off after the curing and smoke for around twenty four hours high above an open fire, or in a home smoker. Hugh Fearnley-Whittingstall is a fountain of knowledge when it comes to making bacon, and I recommend that you invest in his *River Cottage Cook Book* for further enlightened information. The best place to buy your bacon is from a decent butcher. He should be able to tell you what breed it comes from, how the pig was kept and how it was cured. The good stuff is more expensive – you'll just have to eat less. Squashed between two soft slices of plastic white, anointed with a splodge of ketchup and eaten just as the juices soak through the bread, a real bacon butty is as fine a meal as any I know.

Barbecue

It's amazing how a little sun and a small metal box bring out the master chef in every man – or so he thinks. The art of cooking meat, fish or vegetables over a direct charcoal heat is a skilled one, and I wish that the legions of backyard maestros would take this in. Carbonized sausage, napalmed burger and crunchy salmonella chicken (black on the outside, raw within) do not make for a decent, let alone medically safe, lunch whatever the weather. The Americans call our style of barbequing 'grilling'; their 'que' is something different altogether. Real 'Q' involves the slow and low cooking of meat by smoke rather than direct heat. There's an entire industry built around it in the States (especially the South), and it is taken very seriously indeed. Events such as the Jack Daniels Invitational in Lynchburg, Tennessee and Memphis in May sees scores of teams – with names such as Aporkolypse Now, Oink, Cackle and Moo and Swine Dining – compete for prestigious trophies and huge cash prizes. The ingredients of marinades, rubs and mops are closely guarded secrets and the pork, chicken and beef are sometimes truly magnificent. I am now a proud member of the Kansas City Barbecue Society and a Certified Barbecue Judge. This involved chowing my way through around twenty pounds of beef brisket, pulled pork and baby back ribs (as if that wasn't bad enough, I had to cope with the sickly uncertainties of a stinking Bourbon hangover too). A gluttonous day perhaps, but one that will stay with me for the rest of my life. In particular, I remember a pile of pulled pork so juicy, sweet and tender that it could be eaten with a spoon. Barbecue, American style, is a high culinary art. After this grilling, British style, seems a little less exalted.

C for CANNIBALISM

When police raided the house of Jeffrey Dahmer, the "Milwaukee Cannibal", in 1991, they found a freezer packed with human lungs, intestines, kidney and liver. And a store cupboard filled with various bottles, tins and jars. Whilst the body parts are listed in gory detail, we know next to nothing about the condiments. Oregano, cumin and tinned tomatoes, perhaps, for a child con carne? Chillies, coconut milk and fish sauce for a very red curry? Or maybe his cooking skills stretched no further than a jar of 'I Feel Like Bobby Tonight'. Whatever his culinary style, cannibalism remains one of the last taboos, a blood soaked cliché of bubbling pots and vicious savages. Yet cut through the hyperbole and you'll find that, in the vast majority of cases, human meat was not devoured for purely gastronomic reasons, nor savoured for its depth of flavour.

There are, of course, exceptions. The joys of British cuisine held little attraction to a Maori chief named Touai, who was dropped into London society in 1818.

When asked what he missed most about his native islands, he replied that it was '… the feast of human flesh – he was weary of eating roast beef'. But not any old man meat, because '… the flesh of women and children was … the most delicious …' The 19th century Fijians were not so picky about the provenance of their meat, but were particularly keen on heart, thighs and upper arms (all nicely baked of course). The Tartars of the 13th century were partial to the breasts of buxom maidens (only the officers got to sup on this delicacy; the rest had to make do with the chewy dugs of wizened old hags). And certain Nigerian tribes of the 18th century favoured the palms, fingers and toes, believing the 'long pig' to be by far the most succulent of meats (boiled, if you don't mind).

But to early man, human flesh symbolized power, so its consumption was seen to bestow the attributes of the victim upon the snacker; a mere mouthful of thigh meat or chunk of heart might make one stronger, wiser and more powerful. It was a practice common in pre-dynastic Egypt; amongst the much-feared, and fearsomely belligerent Scythians; the Ch'in armies in China; the Ashanti tribes of Africa and the Hurons, Mohawks and Iroquois of Northern America (although cannibalism was also seen as the ultimate insult to the victim, a diss of almighty proportions). And the Aztecs practised human sacrifice and cannibalism on a massive scale, to appease the gods and make sure that the sun rose every day (though some anthropologists argue that they ate human flesh to make up for their lack of a decent herbivore). The Spanish conquistadors were appalled by their bloodthirsty traditions, but appeasing the gods with a still-beating human heart made perfect sense to a society reliant upon a decent crop (the rest of the body was carved up, with the most powerful getting a thigh or liver. The victim's captor would be allowed the off-cuts to make a hearty tlacat-laolli, or maize and man stew). I can understand the revulsion felt by Cortes and his merry band, but they can hardly argue the moral high ground; within ninety years of their arrival, they managed to reduce a population of twenty-five million to a mere one million. But in the majority of these cases, as Reay Tannahill points out in her book *Flesh And Blood: A History Of The Cannibal Culture*, the eating of the human flesh was 'as much a religious rite as the sacrifice itself'.

Another reason, of course, was hunger… extreme, excruciating hunger. As Tannahill notes, 'where there was famine, there was also cannibalism'. The retreat of Napoleon's army from Moscow, the siege of Leningrad and Stalingrad, the 1972 Andean plane crash of the Uruguayan rugby team and the North Korean famine of 1997-8 all drove people to eat flesh of dead friends, colleagues and family – cannibalism was the last option of survival, born out of horrific desperation.

The majority of us would make very bad eating, and I doubt that my flesh could ever be called free-range, let alone organic. In his brilliant satirical essay *A Modest Proposal*, Jonathan Swift argues that babies would be the perfect solution to the Irish Potato Famine. A year old child is 'a most delicious, nourishing, and wholesome food, whether stewed, roasted, baked or boiled: and I make no doubt that it will equally serve in a fricassee, or a ragout.' He has a good point, but your choice slightly depends on whether you like the milk-fed tenderness of a breast-fed baby – and I'm sure a Spanish style marinade of paprika, red wine vinegar, thyme and olive oil would work wonders to the finished dish. – or the slightly more mature flavour of a two or three year old. I asked an eminent London butcher for his views on the matter. After checking that my intentions were scholarly, rather than murderous, he reckoned that an eleven stone male would need about one week of hanging to develop flavour, and the leanest cuts would be…. So what does human hamburger actually taste like? Pork is the general consensus, though Mr. Dahmer was sadly unavailable to comment on the matter. My advice, to anyone with an insatiable appetite for human flesh, is to try Oxford Street. God knows what the hotdog vendors fill their 'sausages' with, but local tramp numbers do seem suspiciously low.

Chillies

Forget the simian rituals of your average 'ten pints and a hot as Hades vindaloo please Sanjay' male; it's pure macho posturing. There's more to chilies than five tablespoons of stale chili powder; smoky serranos as wrinkled as an elephant's scrotum, fiery little bird's eye chillies so beloved of the Thais; the fruity, searing heat of the habaneros; the piquant tabasco, blazing hot with an interesting bite. The list goes on, but as

you may gather I'm a self-confessed chilliholic –
they're pure culinary cocaine.

D for DEEP SOUTH

B eignets, boudin, cracklin', cooter, crawfish, grits, greens, gumbo, etouffe, hush puppies, jamba-laya, muffalettas, pones, po – boys and peach cob-bler... the foods of the Deep South of America roll off the tongue with luscious aplomb. Down home cookin' and Soul food, just two of the region's cuisines, sum up the philosophy of Southern eating. Nothing fancy y'all, just big hearted, pot lickin', belly fillin' fud.

Despite taking in Mississippi, Louisiana, and Alabama, along with the South of Tennessee, the Deep South seems far removed from the rest of the United States. Hundreds of years of slavery, segrega-tion, racial oppression and poverty have left their mark, yet the famed hospitality of the region tran-scends both colour and creed. A history of immigra-tion, both voluntary and enforced, have seen French, British, Spanish and Afro-Caribbean cultures combin-ing to create vibrant, multicultural cuisines. Pig and maize are not only the heart and soul of the region, but the building blocks of American cooking. Legend has it that on a wild Virginian riverbank, back in April 1607, Captains Christopher Newport and John Smith, British sailors who had spent the last twenty one weeks at sea, dropped anchor and came ashore to a place they named Jamestown. And it was here that the Old World porker and New World maize first met, as the seamen sat down to a pow-wow with the resident tribe of Algonquian Indians. The truth is a little less prosaic – the Spanish explorer Hernando de Soto had pigs on board when he landed on the West coast of Florida sixty eight years previously – but it's a romantic story all the same.

The pig is king in these parts, and Soul Food pays mouth-watering homage to the almighty porker. Sheila Ferguson, former lead singer of The Three Degrees and author of *Soul Food – Classic Cuisine from the Deep South*, describes the cuisine as 'soulfully cooked food or richly flavoured foods good for your ever-loving soul'. The native food of the Afro-Caribbean people of America, it was born out of the horrors and iniquities of slavery. Soul Food had its origins in the meagre slave rations of a couple of pounds of bacon or salt pork, a handful of corn and a few local fruits and vegetables. The only place a black slave could hope to express any kind of artistic freedom was in the kitchen of his Colonial master (as well as in his own, rather less well-appointed shacks).

Alongside the plentiful ribs, hams and chops, all parts of the animal are used; fatback (salt pork from the upper side of the pig) or hog jowls are added to Collard greens for extra flavour, and the brains, ears and tail are used to pep up stews and beans; the skin is deep fried to produce gossamer light cracklin', and the small intestine is boiled up to produce chit'lin's (not to all tastes, resembling a slightly porcine chewing gum). And then there's fried chicken, with a golden, crispy crust; the batter offers the merest moment of resistance, before exploding into torrents of sweet juice and a mouthful of white, succulent flesh. 'To cook soul food you must use all of your senses', says Ferguson. But your senses need scant encouragement to revel in it.

Barbecue down here means pork – to my mind the meat most suited to the smokepit (though the Texan beef brisket boys and the mutton maestros down Kentucky way might have a thing or two to say about that). Regional idiosyncrasies abound, arguments rage over the merits of tomato based rather than vinegar-based sauces and whereas one establishment will favour whole hog, another will specialize in shoulder, butt or ribs. But the basic technique remains the same – slo and lo cooked pork (cooked, indirectly, over a fire of various hardwoods, each with their own distinct tang), mopped, injected or rubbed with a whole array of sauces, dry rubs and marinades. This slow cooking allows every fibrous strand of connective tissue to be broken down, so the meat just plops off the bone. Sticky, smoke infused ribs are melt-in-the-mouth tender, piquant and deeply messy – pure swine heaven. Pulled pork sandwiches (from the butt or shoulder) come piled high on soft white bread, slathered in sauce and accompanied by a side of zingy 'slaw.

Breakfast, lunch and dinner, you'll never be far from maize in a myriad of guises; fluffy cornbreads, chewy biscuits (similar to the English scone), hush puppies (deep fried balls of cornmeal, and the perfect partner to fried catfish. Their name is said to have come from their being thrown to dogs by Confederate soldiers to keep the Yankees from finding their camp), pones (basic cornbread) and grits… grits, so loved by Southerners of every colour, but not so loved by me. Bleached cornmeal porridge, with the consistency and taste of wallpaper paste is not an exciting prospect.

'Who's Your Mama, Are You Catholic and Can You Make a Roux?' No one knows Cajun and Creole food like Marcelle Bienvenu, and this wonderfully titled work sums up the spirit of Southern Louisianan cuisine. The Cajun people are the descendants of the French settlers – the Acadians – who were driven out of Nova Scotia by the English in the 1700s. The eerily beautiful bayous in the south of this food-obsessed state became their home, and the bounteous wildlife quickly moved from swamp floor to Cajun cooking pot. The all-important roux (a combination of flour and fat) provides the base for hearty gumbos (a spicy, soup-like stew that can include anything from shrimp and chicken to crawfish, alligator and turtle). Jambalaya is equally sustaining, a one pot mixture of chicken, sausage, ham, vegetables, rice and spice. Tabasco is produced on Avery Island, and the elegant lines of its beautiful bottle grace every table in the state. The Cajuns like their food to have a kick. Roadside signs holler the availability of 'Best Boudin in town', and this spicy sausage, stuffed with pork trimmings and rice, is devoured with gusto. Crawfish are ubiquitous, smothered in onions, bell peppers and celery (known as 'The Trinity' around here), a rich roux and rice as etouffe, or boiled up in vast vats of

seasoned water. These seafood boils are glorious, hands-on orgies of sucking and slurping. Conversation and cutlery have no place here, and the space in front of you quickly becomes a crustacean graveyard, with empty carcasses piled up to your nose.

Creole food, on the other hand, is a little more dignified, the rich city cousin so to speak. At its best in New Orleans, it's an artery-bursting, dairy-drenched beast of a cuisine, matching traditional French cooking techniques with the best of the local produce. Roux plays an equally important role and the Creole gumbo is thickened with okra (gumbo is an African word for okra) rather than Cajun file (ground sassafras leaves); Creole food is generally less robust and spicy, rather more refined. But don't expect anything remotely Nouvelle Cuisine here. Deep fried oysters, platefuls of Eggs Sardou (poached eggs with asparagus and artichokes, drenched in thick Hollandaise sauce), blackened fish, turtle soup, stuffed crab Paradis, frogs' legs en croûte, chicken Clemenceau and soft shell crab po'boys (deep fry the crab and throw them into a baguette with lashings of mayo). Excess is the order of the day and New Orleans institutions such as *Brennan's* specialize in gut-busting, sauce swimming cuisine. Sometimes, though, the unabashed opulence of Creole food is a little overwhelming, even for career gluttons like myself.

Dog

We're quite happy to eat cheap chicken, seemingly oblivious to the fact that these wretched birds spend their short, miserable lives in unimaginable cruelty; packed together in dark, squalid sheds, they barely have room to stretch their wings, let alone wander about of their own free will. And we will merrily devour industrially reared pork all for the sake of cheap bacon. But the moment we hear about a culture alien to our own, chomping down on good old Fido, we're up in arms. Mouths fall open in shock, eyes get dewy and Chicken Macnuggets are dropped in out-rage. 'Those barbarous Koreans/Chinese/Phillipinos are subhuman scum', we cry. 'Put an end to this bar-barous practice', scream the tabloids. Well, hang on a minute. Who are we, with our hypocritical anthropo-morphisation of all things fluffy, to pass judgement on the eating habits of others? In Korea, Southern China and much of South East Asia, as well as parts of Latin America, dog is a much enjoyed, affordable protein source (it's also thought to be an aphrodisiac). If the good citizens of Britain have a problem with that, tough. Breeding dogs for food is no different from rearing any other creature. If the process is a cruel, inhumane one, then every effort should be made to stop it, regardless of the animal involved. I can't say I'm heady with anticipation at the thought of a Labrador stir-fry, but let us look at our own farming practices first, before running to condemn the tastes of others.

E for ENGLISH FOOD

For a nation obsessed with heritage and history, we show a criminal disregard for our national cuisine. So much so, in fact, that we've started to believe the hackneyed stereotypes, perpetuated by our sneering Continental cousins, of a land filled with bland, stodgy puddings – both human and suet based – and overcooked, disease ridden meat. English food, they moan to anyone who will listen, lacks imagination, flair, finesse and passion. It is, in short, a laughing stock; the fat, spotty bespectacled kid that cowers in the corner of the culinary classroom. English cuisine may not be as refined as French food, or as intricately spiced as Thai or Indian, but it can be equally delectable. It is a fine cuisine in its own right.

But some of the criticisms have sound foundation. We seem to have lost our collective sense of taste. We're happy to put up with pappy tomatoes, mundane meat and insipid apples, just as long as they're cheap – although lack of cash is no excuse for shoddy eating, as Jane Grigson pointed out in *English Food*, '… let them not plead poverty as an excuse for bad food' [when they spend so much on hard liquor, gambling, ice cream of a worthless kind, sweets, cakes, biscuits ..]' – But flavour does seem an unimportant afterthought to us, as long as every tomato or apple looks unblemished, shiny and round. The supermarkets boast of bringing us imported strawberries all the year, seemingly oblivious to the fact that the eating of British produce in season should be central to our enjoyment of real food.

Thanks, in part, to the omnipotence of the supermarkets, we've lost contact with the source of our food. If it says 'steak' on the vacuum packed, cellophane sealed package, who cares where it comes from, how it was reared, what it ate and for how long it was hung? It's just another faceless, generic product, bearing scant relation to those cud-chewing cuties that pepper our country fields. The supermarkets want to distance us from the mucky reality of death, blood and guts, as if the meat arrived in this world ready wrapped. The low price of this meat comes at a high humanitarian cost. For the time being, the supermarkets have succeeded in cutting us off from our culinary roots, by tapping into an apathy about and ignorance of our native produce. But hidden within our stiff-upper lipped bodies is a gourmand waiting to escape. And oh-so-slowly, we're just beginning to rediscover the glories of English cuisine.

Our food is about warmth, comfort and pure pleasure. When the nights are dark, stormy and thick with winter clichés, we want basic, well-sourced tucker that fills the belly and warms the cockles of the heart. Its strength lies in its straightforward simplicity and honesty of flavour. To dislike English food because it isn't spicy enough, or lacks the contrast or texture of Chinese food, is to miss the point. We should take the cuisine on its own merits, rather than looking for things that it lacks. It is not, and never will be a complex haute cuisine, but it's none the worse for that. Unlike French food, our cuisine springs from the domestic, rather than chef-led, tradition. And it was cooks like Hannah Glasse, Eliza Acton and, up to a point, Mrs Beeton (a little too economically minded for my taste) who led the way. Of course, our country had been invaded by Celts, Picts, Romans, Vikings, Saxons, Angles and Normans – and that was just up to 1066. All left a culinary mark, but none actually changed our fundamental love of simplicity (though the highly spiced aristocratic food of medieval times, with the emphasis on sweet and sour, might seem a little alien to our modern tastes). And the past sixty years or so have seen the immigrant West Indians and Asians bringing their own vibrant influences to our cooking.

Of course, the finest, most straightforward food is that made with the best ingredients, something that our sceptred isle has in abundance. Our culinary strength lies in raw materials, and to find these, you have to seek out the specialist producers, the people who put flavour first. Our temperate climate provides lush grass for our livestock, fertile fields for our crops, shady orchards and bountiful vegetable gardens. And, as Dorothy Hartley laconically points out in *Food in England*, 'England is an island entirely surrounded by fish'. Yet we only eat a tiny percentage of what is available to us. Nothing, to my mind, beats a fresh

Cromer crab for sweet succulence, or the saline sexiness of a Colchester Native Oyster. The tiny brown shrimp has more flavour in its minute body than the fleshy tiger prawn could ever dream of. And a plateful of smoked eel, accompanied by a mountain of pungent horseradish is as much a taste sensation as a green papaya salad or Goan vindaloo. If there is a guiding ethos, it is let the flavours speak for themselves.

Look what the English have brought to the international culinary round table. We invented afternoon tea, with its mass of rich fruit cakes, airy sponge cakes, fluffy scones slathered thick with Cornish clotted cream and piquant raspberry jam and crumpets awash with golden butter. Delicate cucumber sandwiches (crusts off, of course), luscious chocolate cakes and every variety of tea leaf under the sun. And the great, glorious English breakfast, a meal that would knock out the insipid continental version with a single punch. It might not be exactly what the doctor ordered, but when it tastes this good, who cares? It's a meal enjoyed by every class of society, from builder's bacon butty to aristo's grand country sideboard groaning with bacon, eggs, sausage, kedgeree (an Anglo-Indian import), devilled kidneys, smoky fleshed kippers, cold grouse and black pudding. Substitute scummy Danish bacon, battery eggs and sphincter sausages, and it becomes the grease-filled Seventh circle of hell. But use well-made, traditional English ingredients, and there's nothing that I'd rather eat. These aren't mere meals, but wonderful national institutions, of which we should be rightfully proud.

And we're masters of the roast, of baking, of succulent pies and pudding, stuffed with all manner of beautiful filling. The reason we suffer from such poor PR, as in the case of breakfasts, is that we try to cut corners and save money. When you do this, the poor reputation of English cuisine is not without foundation. Gristly steak mixed with a few desultory hunks of un-trimmed, urine-scented kidney and cooked in a cloying brown liquid of flour and grease is not a steak and kidney pudding – it's just depressing. You need tough cuts of meat, sure, but cooked slowly so they release all their deep flavour. And the kidneys must offer a wonderful contrast of texture, especially when eaten with a forkful of chewy, suet pastry. The liquor should be dark, rich and intensely meaty, a complement, rather than a hindrance, to the pudding as a whole. And how can we sing about the glories of the Melton Mowbray pork pie when we're peddled artificially pink flesh encased in a turgid, grease-infused coffin? Dickinson and Morris hand-raise their pies, using homemade, jellied stock and local pork. Everything is done by hand, and the end result, to quote Michael Winner, is nothing short of 'historic'. I could go on endlessly, about fish with a Kevlar coating and soggy chips, as opposed to virgin white flesh, wrapped in a golden, gossamer batter. And double-blanched chips, cooked in beef dripping. We have the recipes, but all too often we let everything down with insensitive sourcing and lazy cooking.

But the situation is improving, and we're beginning to let our presence be known once more. We're moving away from over-processed rubbish, and starting to rediscover the wonders of our cuisine. Awards such as The Great Taste Awards judge on flavour, rather than price and packaging. And uncompromising food heroes across the country are still fighting for the small, local producer. How can we ignore the mellow charms of an oozing Stinking Bishop, or the more 'bitey' depth of a perfectly aged Montgomery or Keen's cheddar? Stilton remains one of the grand old men of the cheese world, with its incredible richness and seductive crumbly texture. Imagine life without crispy, crunchy crackling, or slices of properly hung, longhorn beef. Not forgetting a fluffy Yorkshire pud and mountains of purple sprouting for winter warming. Or cottage pie, cooked so the potato crust is just golden, served with a plateful of peas. Summer sees a butterflied leg of lamb, barbecued until just charred, then served with a light, green garden salad. Or a freshly boiled crab, just picked and still warm. And a bowlful of Morecambe Bay potted shrimps, with the merest hint of lemon juice and crusty brown bread. Great, juicy coils of Cumberland sausage please the eye and palate, along with vast sides of York or Bradenham hams. Fried elvers, gulls' eggs and celery salt, roast grouse with braised red cabbage, thin gravy and game chips and a pheasant casserole, rich with game and pleasure, all show off the glories of simple, seasonal food, while smoked Wiltshire back bacon, honest robust black pudding and roast mutton with caper sauce are testament to our winning ways with meat. Apple pie, treacle tart (with a slowly melting lump of fresh vanilla ice cream), rhubarb crumble (that lip puckering tartness) vie with summer pudding and zingy pond pudding – its whole lemon hidden within – for the title of Queen of Puddings (although there is a custard, jam and meringue concoction that already lays claim to that particular title). Just-cut asparagus in May, so fresh that they're still sweet are too good to mess up with anything more than melted butter or a sharp vinaigrette. Or a Dover sole, grilled with the merest brush of butter. Look at the list, then look me in the eye. Can you seriously tell me that English food is bland and mundane? I agree that the cooking and ingredients often let the side down, but we have to start instilling a love of food, as well as proper cooking techniques, in young children. They hold the future in their hands, and while the occasional bag of Monster Munch or Macdonald's cheese burger is perfectly acceptable, it shouldn't become the norm. I love English food, not at the expense of other cuisines, but alongside them. And next time you get culinary abuse from a foreign friend, stand proud, gird your upper lip and fight them to the death.

Elvers

These writhing, translucent worms might not look too appetizing when alive, as well as having enough slime and ooze to send a myxophobic running for his shrink, but quickly fried in bacon fat and beaten eggs, the baby eels (or glass eels) are a true English delicacy. Of course, they're a real rarity too, as we export every single one of these wriggling beauties to Spain, France and Portugal. In these countries which wor-ship the elvers they are brought sizzling to the table with garlic and chili. It's very hard to find them over here, but if you ask around the Severn area, when the tides are high enough, in April or May, you might get lucky. Or you might get a punch in the face. Because these slippery blighters can fetch up to £170 per kilo, the elver fishermen, who fish at night with torches – are understandably secretive. So if you want to check out a highlight of English cuisine, with its subtle, velvety fishiness, I suggest that you get on a plane to somewhere that appreciates the elver's true gastronomic worth.

F for FAST FOOD

Fast Food might seem an odd inclusion for a book so vehemently opposed to tasteless, over-processed muck, but bear with me. Of course, not all fast food is junk food. A sandwich piled high with thick, pink slices of York ham, nestled in between two hunks of butter smeared, home-made bread, and anointed with streaks of pungent Colman's mustard is fast food. As is Thai green Papaya Salad, where shreds of cool, crunchy papaya blend with salty fish sauce, sweet palm sugar, sour lemon juice and nuclear powered prik kii nuu suan (or mouse shit) chilies all combine to create something utterly sublime. And in countries where freshly cooked and boldly flavoured street food is part of the culinary culture, fast food is cheap, filling and generally delicious. But as Britain's contemporary contribution to street food starts and ends with the Oxford Street hotdog, we have to look elsewhere for our speedy eats.

Fish and chips are a glorious British institution; their finest, equal to any other fast food around the world. Fresh fish, briefly dipped in a beer batter, then fried to golden, so the flesh steams inside its crispy shell, is one of the great pleasures of our cuisine. Cooking fish like this is a dying art, though, and it's a delicacy that you have to search for. But when it comes to fast food, we look to America for inspiration, as well as for blame.

Burger, hotdog and fried chicken is the quintessentially American trilogy of foods, and examples range from the divine to the unspeakable. Where these are concerned I'm fairly dictatorial in my tastes. When it comes to burgers, I want good quality meat, minced, with a fairly high fat content to keep it juicy. A little cheese and bacon are an acceptable embellishment, along with tomato, lettuce and gherkin. And that's it. The first bite should consist of tender meat, just-browned bun and a rivulet of juice down the chin. Forget those 'look-at-me, I'm a twat' burger 'deconstructions' that were so popular in New York at the start of last year. I love foie gras, and Kobe beef, but I don't want them in my burger. Let's leave these preening pretenders to the Masters of the Universe, who can eat their concoctions with a hefty side order of irony.

A hot dog too is an object of veneration and a genuine American hotdog means a frankfurter; a British style sausage in a bun is a good snack, but not a hotdog. A two-block walk in Manhattan becomes a calorie fuelled minefield, as I'm unable to pass a hotdog stand without stopping and munching. I relish the rituals of topping the dog with sauerkraut, Crayola yellow mustard and ketchup. And the first mouthful, that offers the thrilling contrast of soft bun, sharp condiment and tight skinned frank. Those soggy horse cocks offered in the majority of British cinemas are an affront to a noble part of the fast food pantheon, and not even worth noting here, save to say 'avoid at all costs.'

Genuine Southern fried chicken bears no resemblance to the flabby, listless flesh of KFC. I once found a hot chicken shack in a less than salubrious part of Nashville, Tennessee, which blew my mind, in more ways than one (the sauce was pretty fierce.) The batter was light and crunchy, the chicken plump and bursting with juice. Again, it's a toothsome combination of brittle batter and yielding meat that makes it so memorable.

But when it comes to any discussion of fast food chains, I tend to go quietly. Why? Because I'm a little embarrassed. I may hate KFC, for its sins against good taste, chicken and the South, but I have a weakness for MacDonald's. Burger King, I can live without. I know that their burgers taste a little – and a Lilliputian little at that – more 'genuine' than Maccee Dee's, but I always feel like I've just swallowed a fat child. It sits in the stomach for days, like a lump of flame grilled lead. Macdonald's, on the other hand, has that miraculously brief period of satisfaction, quickly followed by an urge for more. Their fries are crisper, and their cheese burgers rock. There's nothing genuine about this ultimate snack item; it just tastes of MacDonald's. It's something about that sickly sweet bun, the 'cheese' that sticks to the roof of your mouth, and the perky gherkin, that I can't get enough of. I've managed to cut down my consumption to about one a month, but there are certain hangovers that only MacDonald's can cure. I hate what the company stands for, but I love their cheese burger. And there's the rub. I'm a man driven by my stomach, and when it comes to the showdown between conscience and craving, the latter usually comes off best. If I were a stronger person, I'd walk past those Golden Arches of multi-national imperialism and sneer knowingly. As it is, I creep in, order the burger, wolf it down in one, and slink out, burger breathed and full of joy.

Foie gras

As I've just said, when it comes down to conscience versus craving, it's craving that usually kicks con-science's butt. But when it comes to eating foie gras, the artificially engorged liver of the duck or goose, I don't feel even the merest prickle of guilt. Not a tick-le. Because the bird did not waddle off this mortal coil to become some flavour-free, deep-frozen chunk of cheap protein, it died to produce one of the true glories of gastronomy. Ok, so the process of creating foie gras could never be described as entirely humane. The goose or duck is force fed, by means of a long metal tube jammed down its throat, large amounts of maize about three times a day. After three weeks of enforced dining, our feathered friends are killed, and the vast liver is either sold whole and raw – briefly fried, it's one of the richest, most decadent mouthfuls there is – cooked or semi-cooked and preserved in tins and glass jars. The best, in my view, comes from Strasbourg or South West France, although Israel and some Eastern

European countries provide the extra quantities demanded by those guzzling aficionados.

But the birds, unlike intensively farmed chickens or pigs, are treated like quacking royalty. After all, the farmer's income depends on the good health of the bird and a sick or maltreated bird will not produce a decent liver. When this organ is worth more than ten times the rest of the bird, it's very much in the farmer's interest to keep it happy. And despite what you may have read to the contrary, I've come across numerous accounts that vouch for their day to day wellbeing. In fact, they seem lavished with love and attention. Stephanie Alexander, in *Cooking And Travelling In South West France* watched a goose being fed in Sorges '…and saw no flapping of wings or squawking, attempts to avoid Mr. Maynard's arm, widening of eyes or any other overt signs of distress.' Anyway, I believe that the means justifies the gastronomic end. In the words of Charles Gerard, in *L'Ancienne Alsace à Table*, 'The goose is nothing, but man has made it an instrument for the output of a marvellous product, a kind of living hothouse in which there grows the supreme fruit of gastronomy.'

G for GROUSE

I'm quite happy to leave the killing of grouse to enthusiasts and experts. It's not that I have any moral objection to shooting. Far from it; if we didn't shoot, how else could we get our hands on these wonderfully juicy little birds? Besides, shooting is essential to the economic, environmental and social fabric of the countryside. No, the reason that I'm loth to pick up a gun is because I'm a piss-poor shot. I'm not being falsely modest here, putting down my Purdey prowess to seem humble and self-effacing. I really stink. Even the pheasant, one of the dullest witted of birds, worked out that flying over my peg would mean a few hours reprieve from the Aga.

My father, on the other hand, is a true dead eye dick, the kind of man who can circumcise a gnat with a spud gun. From five hundred yards. So rather than pepper the air with impotent lead, I just aimed at his birds. Although he quickly got wise to the scam, it was a face-saver – on both sides – to share the glory. My other main problem with shooting was the early start. Every Saturday morning, from an early age, I was dragged from the soft, warm folds of my bed and forced to face the sullen, pasty mediocrity of early British morning, then spend the rest of the day, freezing my toes off in some godforsaken field. The only break was a hearty lunch, where mouthfuls of steaming hotpot would be interrupted by, 'So old boy, are you looking forward to joining the army like your dad?' Yeah right. I adored nattering away with my father, but always longed to spend my Saturdays in London, smoking, drinking and hunting an entirely superior species of bird.

But at least when it came to shooting pheasants, you weren't required to move much. No such indolence was permitted when it came to grouse. As my idea of rigorous exercise consisted of leaving the sofa to press fast forward on the video – only, of course, when the remote was out of batteries – the idea of walking up grouse was enough to make me swoon with exertion (proper grouse shoots are driven by beaters, but, for obvious reasons, I wasn't let loose on these). We would trudge through the heather (which would invariably end up spiking me through my socks), guns at the ready, waiting for the tell tale flurry of tiny wings. Except when they did arrive, I missed them all. It didn't take me long to work out that when it came to grouse, I was best armed with knife and fork.

Tucking into the first grouse of the season is a much anticipated event, as they are the finest tasting of all game. Hanging them for a few days intensifies their gamey tang quite beautifully, but if you do this keep an eye on them. I usually leave them a day too long, only to find the birds crawling with tiny maggots. But an old friend recommends throwing them in the oven the moment they are shot; the flavour is rather more delicate, but equally enjoyable. Grouse taste finest in August. As the season wears on, they become tough and stringy. Freezing the bird might lose you a touch of succulence, but at least it preserves that incredible flavour. It's also too good to sully with anything else but roasting (although the dried up old pensioners can be stewed in a casserole). And it must be served with fluffy bread sauce, crispy game chips and a small lake of glistening, consommé like gravy. I want mine just pink, and after slicing elegant slivers off the breast, I rip off the legs and pick them clean. That way, you don't miss any shard or shred of sumptuous flesh. By the time I've finished, the tiny carcass is gleaming as if it had spent two hundred years under the Kalahari sun. They're surprisingly filling for their size, though the height of luxury, for me, is a cold grouse for breakfast the next morning, shot, of course, by someone else and preferably served to me in bed.

Goat's cheese

I've never licked a filth-stained, concrete lined pig sty floor. But if I did, I'm convinced that it would taste of goat's cheese. It's a food that disgusts me so much that I cannot even watch someone else eat it. Even the mildest, fresh flavoured specimens like Saint Claude possess that unmistakeable ammonia tang that loiters in the mouth like a pee-stained tramp. Admittedly, the flavour is more dirty udders – and no, my tongue has been nowhere near these either – than farmyard floor, but the essence is there. The truly pungent varieties, though, are plain offensive. This abject hatred is rather irrational, as I love any and every kind of cheese (save Primula and cottage cheese), and on the few times that I've tasted goat's milk, have never had a problem. I really want to love goat's cheese, to frolic among those ashy pyramids and leafy logs. I long to talk sourness, bite and body with anyone who will listen but every time I see a perfectly respectable salad sullied by a couple of oozing, pure white discs, I despair. I just can't do it. It's also the most underhand of cheeses, creeping up on you in seemingly innocuous tarts, canapés and salads. One moment, you're merrily filling your mouth, the next, you're frantically searching for a convenient place to spit it all out again. Goat's cheese and me? An affair never meant to be.

H for HUNGER

Hunger is a bit-player in most people's lives, the
small but essential walk-on role that keeps the
action moving smoothly. To me, though, it plays a
rather larger part, the demanding, limelight-loving
diva that's rarely sated for a second. And I'm totally
in thrall to its every whim and urge. Of course, I
know nothing of real hunger, thanks to a fortunate
accident of birth. But six years spent behind high rus-
set walls, at a cushy prep school on the outskirts of
Oxford, was enough to transform a healthy appetite
into a raging greed, an all-consuming obsession
fuelled by half a dozen years of filth.

Before prep-school, my appetites were healthy. And
hunger was, as it is supposed to be, little more than
an instinctive reaction to an empty stomach. If food at
the local day school was rank and choleric – and it
invariably was, save for tomato soup and stale
baguettes after swimming on Tuesdays – there was
always the thought of tea at home to keep the tummy
quiet. Boiled eggs and soldiers, streaky bacon, silky

poached haddock, cottage pies and peas were all hoovered up and taken for granted. Besides, I was never far from a restorative Fizzbomb, soothing Pacer or tongue-tingling Sherbet DipDab (far preferable to the Sherbet Fountain, thanks to the strawberry lolly) to take the edge off any raging pang. Good food was always a given in my family; proper local meat came from Love and Son in Corsham, glistening fish from the fishmonger and fresh vegetables from the garden. Purple sprouting, pink Fir Apple potatoes and baby broad beans were seasonal, staple items at home. And there always seemed to be something bubbling, stewing or rising in or on the Aga, along with endless cake mix bowls to lick and polish. To say that my mother was at the heart of all this, spoon in hand and pinny tied, would be somewhat of an overstatement. When it comes to roasts of any kind, along with baked eggs, grilled fish, sauté potatoes and perfectly poised salads, she is in a league of her own. But puddings, pastry, freezer filling and baking were best left to those that actually enjoyed it, so we always had a part-time cook. They ranged from the sublime – Bridget with her chewy meringues and epic Treacle Tarts – to the less than inspiring, although I always went to bed with belly filled. Suddenly, just shy of eight, the homely clichés were shattered when I was packed off to prep-school. And hunger, in all its sharp-toothed viciousness, took hold.

We all know that school food is bad. It's a universal experience, and the subject of many a second-rate joke. But the sheer lack of flavour, allied with a remarkable disregard for anything resembling quality ingredients, blew me away. Breakfast was bad enough; cold, cardboard toast, scummy, pallid flaps of bacon, glistening with sinister grease. Fried eggs with the consistency of chewing gum, and a faint, fishy tang. Garish fried bread that concealed a pint of fat within its spongy folds. And pink, slippery sausages that made no effort to cover up their journey from the slaughterhouse floor; arseholes, eyelids and the odd toenail. This tawdry collection of barnyard bits bore no relation to the mighty breakfast of my recent memory. By 8.15 am, I was already ravenous. But this wretched meal was positively lavish compared to the next two. Grey, gristly mince was the ubiquitous protein of choice. They sometimes decided to add a sticky mass of overcooked pasta and call it Bolognese. Or throw in a few hunks of undercooked onion and come up with … mince and onion. Or top it with cold, lumpy mashed potato –which stuck to the roof of your mouth – and call it Shepherd's Pie. Or mix in a couple of sheets of sodden pasta, top it with plastic cheddar and name it Lasagne. All were equally chilling, and fundamentally inedible. And my hunger burned all the more brightly. Boiled potatoes were rarely far from the table, complete with obligatory black bits and rock hard centre. Our fish pie was an unpalatable mass of spiny bones and floury white sauce. Dried up old faggots, diseased liver thick with impenetrable veins and pork chops that tasted like chipboard all vied for the title of worst ever, along with salt-lick gammon, complete with cloying ring of tinned pineapple. Supper was more of the same, save for the occasional treat such as canned ravioli, beans on toast and the much loved 'rib' (or a piece of mechanically shaped processed pork, dyed brick red with noxious 'e-numbers' and shaped into a Dairy Milk bar sized hunk). The good things, though, were always in short supply and my nights were filled with foodie wet dreams, gleaned from the pages of everything from *National Geographic* to Billy Bunter and *The Magic Faraway Tree*.

Sunday was the worst of all. Not only did you have to sit through chapel, but also had to endure a sullied and defiled version of Sunday lunch. The fervent imaginations of Pasolini and Ballard combined could not have come close to this noxious vision of carnivore hell. The meat was pre-sliced, pre-cooked and arrived swimming on a wave of brackish piss. The species of animal was guessed not by flavour, but colour; muddy brown for beef, grey for lamb and beige for pork. The taste, what little there was, was identical in every case. Vegetables sat stewing in a gassy, soupy slop of yellowing dishwater, while the potatoes were our old favourites, the boiled buggers, splashed with a couple of flicks of oily brown varnish and called 'roasted'. The hours following saw me at my lowest ebb. Because we now had five hours to kill, five hours in which I wandered the school, consumed by hunger. I'd make matters worse by heading to the library and drooling over sumptuous photographs of American feasts in heavy Time Life Foods of the World. I fantasized over pictures of Chinese wedding feasts, heavy with soothing noodle soups, bowls of sticky rice and vast hunks of barbecued pork. I got to know about hearty cassoulets, crispy confit of duck and paellas so rich and vivid that I nearly licked the page. And all this was available to those lucky people on the other side of the wall. It was gastro masturbation, made all the worse by the prospect of a Spartan Sunday supper; just a bag of crisps, a few slices of bread and, if we were very lucky, an Orange Club. Sunday supper was, after all, supposed to be a treat.

This ever-present knowing hunger even found its way into the classroom. If a biology experiment involved chewing a piece of bread – something to do with saliva breaking up food – I'd always try and nick an extra slice. The same with apples, fractions and maths lessons. Only the thrice weekly sweet ration provided anything to look forward to. Chewits were best, although Curly Wurlies, Refreshers, Stinger Bars and Highland Toffee were decent alternatives. Ruffle Bar, a sickly combination of bright pink coconut encased in a cheap chocolate filling, was widely agreed as the sweetie nadir. Coolmints once made a memorable appearance, but it seemed the authorities were unaware of their laxative properties. Within hours, the school erupted into a stinking mess of Swiftian excess, and Coolmints were never seen again. During Lent, we were 'encouraged' to hand in our cherished ration in aid of starving children. A box sat at the entrance to the dining hall, and we were supposed to deposit our swag within. Quite how a tube of American Hardgums would solve the famine problem I don't know, but I quickly became adept at a Houdini-like sleight of hand. To any casual observer, it looked like Parker Bowles had handed over the goods – all the while it was carefully concealed in my Guernsey sleeve.

My constant hunger was quickly turning to greed, and I looked to other, more underhand ways of getting my fix. It started when some foolish soul left his locker door open, revealing a packet of strawberry Chewits for all who cared to look. The temptation was too much, and I snuck back in later to filch the lot. From then on, nothing edible was safe from my sticky little paws. I was honourable though – I never stole from friends unless I was really starving. My biggest ever cache nearly turned out to be my downfall. Snooping around a teacher's desk one evening, I came across a drawer filled with unimaginable riches; Mars Bars, Marathons, Twixes and Milky Ways were just the beginning. Rather than dip in now and again, I swiped the whole lot, hiding them around the grounds to collect later. The next day, the headmaster called an assembly and told us all about the devious, filthy little thief in our midst. 'I know, of course, who did it', he spluttered, 'but I want the boy to own up by himself'. I was well wise to this ruse, and kept my mouth shut, even joining in the frantic whispering as to who was the culprit. But as no one saw me do it, I knew I was in the clear. The whole school got detention for my sheer, dishonest greed, and I apologize to any of you who suffered for my sins. They did, by the way, taste very, very sweet.

So by methods foul and fair, food became the centre of my life. There was no tuck shop, and smuggled food carried hefty punishment. Not that that stopped me, although a carefully concealed stash was usually polished off on the first night back. I'd spend hours washing teachers' cars for half a king-sized Mars Bar, grow mustard, cress and carrots in my tiny patch of garden, and guard the seedlings with my life.

Public school, after 6 years of near starvation, was sheer bliss. If you define greed as a desire for food without the actual need for it, then I was a textbook example. After the enforced celibacy of the food at prep school, public school seemed like an orgy of free love and easy eats. Suddenly, I could drink all the Coke I wanted, Sodastream to my heart's content and eat when I chose. Food in my house was the best in the school, thanks to a passionately foodie housemaster. It was edible, sometimes even acceptable, and he introduced me to the fiery joys of dried Kashmiri chilies. But who needs school food when the tuck shop was just a few moments waddle away. It was called Rowland's and I fell in love with its rather utilitarian charms. Presided over by the chain-smoking, fearsome Carole – who actually had a heart of pure marshmallow – it was Eton's answer to Xanadu. It opened at Chamber's, our eleven o clock break, and the glass warming cabinet would be piled high with crusty buns, stained yellow on the inside with melted butter, and filled with two rashers of perfectly cooked bacon. I'd fight through the scrum, hands aloft, with just one phrase on my lips. 'Bacon with, please, Mrs Cripps'. If you caught her eye in time – no mean feat when you were fighting with thirty similarly obsessed teenage boys – one of those golden rolls was yours. Sausage rolls were good, but came a poor second to bacon. And cheese and ham rolls were the next rung down. I'd also stock up on penny sweets for the two lessons between break and lunch. They had 'em all. The modern classics were kept in a counter at the front of the shop; milk gums that stained your black waistcoat with a tell-tale white smudge, fizzy cola bottles so sharp that they gave you pimples on your tongue (like the old style Pickled Onion Monster

Munch RIP), mouth blackening BlackJacks and perennially popular Fruit Salads. Then billowy Flumps, Sour Apples, foam shrimps and bananas, very retro sherbet flying saucers (that you'd let dissolve on the tongue), aniseed balls, white mice (very dodgy chocolate), Jelly Snakes and chunky Refreshers (the chewy, rather than hard version). The old school classics were lined up in glass jars at the back of the shop. You bought them by the quarter, and nothing was left out. Cola Cubes, sherbet lemons, Extra Strong Mints (good for covering smoky breath), Cough Drops, aniseed twist (too grown up for my liking), bonbons, yellow, white and pink, all dusted with icing sugar and rhubarb and custard. On Saturdays, the range included microwave chips, hamburgers and hotdogs, as well as pints of Brown Cow (Coke with a block of cheap vanilla mixed in. It looked like a polluted stream, but tasted blissful). With the television tuned to Baywatch, and a few coins for the F1 Driving machine burning a hole in my pocket, I didn't think life could get any better.

I quickly found out that sports could be avoided. I'm terminally mal-co-ordinated, so whiled away many happy hours in Rowlands. And my tummy began to grow. This wasn't helped by the arrival of Tap, the school pub. In the final two years, we were deemed sufficiently mature to drink. The limit was two pints per boy, but as I got ratted on a half of shandy, it was never an issue. And as is befitting for the older teenager, the snacks got more sophisticated. Suddenly, Chambers became a feast of hot sausages dipped in pungent English mustard, halved avocados filled with vinaigrette and plump prawn rolls, rosy with Marie Rose sauce. It took a few months of dysentery in India to rob me of my belly, but my greed, mercifully, escaped unscathed. As to cold showers, buggery, bullying and cornflake wedgies, I knew little. But after ten years of expensive education, I did learn one thing. I was, and still am, a greedy little bugger.

I for ICE LOLLY

You might think me a little childish for preferring the Day-Glo charms of the ice lolly over the rather more refined comforts of ice cream. But too much is written in praise of this frozen pudding, and not enough in support of the lolly. I like mine as sickly sweet, naff and garish as possible, and if it stains my tongue nuclear pink, then all the better. Because unlike ice cream, where homemade is usually best, the greatest lollies are those stuffed with a noxious smorgasbord of exotic e-numbers. And although I bang on with utter seriousness about the values of fresh, well-sourced food, when it comes to lollipops, I'm a self-confessed hypocrite.

I've always found the homemade variety too watery. Like cheap Slush Puppies, you spend two seconds sucking out the cold juice and are left with a deeply boring chunk of ice. Worse still are the ghastly varieties, such as the Solero. With their branded sticks and 'grown-up' flavours, they're not iced lollies at all – just insufferably smug. It's been a bad time for lollipop lovers over the last ten years. For every lip-smacking success – the Fruit Pastille ice lolly, with its different flavoured rings, and the Jelly Baby with a wobbling jelly centre – there have been a deluge of second-rate frozen snacks that would not have lasted a moment in the endless summer days of the late Seventies, the true golden age of the ice lolly.

We view our youth through raspberry tinted glasses, and the flavours that we loved so much aged seven seem positively repellent now. But many of the old classics have long since disappeared, allowing them to remain eternally exciting. The local shop near my grandparents' house was the focal point of our daily life, and the Lyons Maid logo, of three rather odd-looking children engaged in a merry dance, was engraved upon my heart. They were heady days indeed, where every visit had the possibility of a new flavour. Best of all was the Superman cola flavoured lolly, with plastic stick. As you licked away the layers of fizzy brown ice, a plastic figure would slowly emerge. Not only was it the best tasting cola flavour in existence –and I swear it used to fizz in my mouth – but it also meant that I could suck and crunch with indiscriminate ease. Why? Because I have a slight phobia of wooden lolly sticks. I dreaded the moment where my tongue hit the wood, and it still makes my mouth pucker to think about it. I'm convinced it had something to do with its similarity to the tongue poker so beloved by doctors. But with such a dazzling profusion of flavours, my passion for the popsicle far outweighed my bizarre disgust of their stick.

My choice depended on my mood at the time. For alcoholic kicks, I'd go with the soft orange and red waves of the Tequila Sunrise. Or for adult refreshment, the Cider Barrel never disappointed. Although they contained no booze at all, we'd wander around afterwards, convinced that we were drunk (it must have been an 'e-number' related rush). The Cider Barrel had a similar effect, though the best were always bought from the ice-cream van. We used to sneer at Orange Maids and Mivvis (or Splits, depending on the brand), as my mother ate them and they seemed depressingly grown up. But the contrast between cool, strawberry shell and creamy vanilla is one that I've come to love (leave the Pineapple splits alone though – they're rank). Zooms, with their thrusting shape, are still around today, although the banana bit was, and still is, frustratingly thin and could be licked off in a matter of seconds to reveal a rather more mundane raspberry section. Fab, too, can still be found, though it seems like a washed out shadow of its former self. Named after Lady Penelope's number plate (FAB 1), it was a chunk of strawberry ice, with vanilla ice cream and a top covered with hundreds and thousands. Once you'd dealt with this, the blood red remains were less exciting. Happy Days, named after the American sitcom, was another classic; I perfected stripping away the super sweet sugar bobbles on top, as well as the strawberry ice cream, to just be left with the chocolate bar centre. You could treat a Big Feast in the same way. Big Foot was more ice cream than lolly, and tended to melt very quickly while the Mini Milk was perfect for comfort, and in spite of having minimal milk content, was acceptable to mothers as a healthy treat.

The Eighties had their fair share of classics too; the

Tangle Twister had wonderfully creamy tropical ice-cream bands, mixed with lime sorbet. You could lick away the ice cream, to be left with just sorbet stripes and the red slush inside. And the Calippo, with its revolutionary cardboard sheath, shot to the top of my charts, thanks to its lack of stick. Orange was always best, although the strawberry ones available in Europe at the time gave us whole minutes of hilarity; it you sucked it right, you could recreate the lipstick shape of our dog's willy. Moving it in and out of its cardboard home made it all the more realistic. But it was the arrival of the Mars Bar ice cream – too rich by far – that blew the competition out of the water, and suddenly no one seemed to care about us lolly lovers. So sadly it may be time to put away childish things, and move onto the grown up Magnum. On second thoughts, this lolly lover is not for turning.

Insects

'What is repulsive in one part of the world, in another is simply lunch'. Jerry Hopkins makes a pertinent point in his book *Strange Foods*. Insects have long ceased to be an important form of nutrition in the West and the nearest we'll ever get to eating them here is either a mistakenly swallowed fly or a chocolate covered 'novelty' scorpion. A quick search through the internet could find you Cheddar worm crisps (oven-baked, not fried!), cans of ants' eggs and deep fried crickets. But these are gastro-gags, the sort of thing that those cheap gadget catalogues, that slip so readily out of the Sunday papers, would call a 'conversation piece'. They're nothing more than an over-priced, ghoulish joke. The fact that the chocolate is cheap and waxy and the insect filling plain and dusty means that you won't be queuing up for more. In some parts of the world, though, insects are seen as a plentiful, nutritious and free source of sustenance. And entomophagists (who study the insect as food) have long argued their merits. The roasted abdomen of the Parasol or leaf cutting ant is supposed to taste like crispy bacon, the honey pot ant of Australia has a sweet tangy flavour. And ant eggs are eaten with beer in Laos and Northern Thailand, popping in the mouth and releasing a creamy substance said to be similar in taste to Camembert. That said, I once tried something that looked like deep-fried locusts in Thailand – there wasn't any real flavour, aside from the fiery dipping sauce, and I remember having to pick bits of leg from my teeth for hours to come. Even if we get over the initial revulsion of eating a bug, they're just not interesting to most Western palates, or necessary to our diet. We may laugh and grimace at the perceived insect-chewing antics of our Asian, African and Australasian cousins. But that doesn't stop us slathering insect secretion over our toast every morning. Described in these cold, scientific terms, even our beloved honey sounds a little, well, distasteful.

J for JEWISH FOOD

'You don't like your pastrami, honey? You'll fade away.' With that, the ancient waitress began to clear the battle-soiled Formica table. Her hair was piled high, taller even than the vast meat, bread and mustard monolith that sat, untouched, before me and fiercely lacquered to within an inch of its life. I grunted a response through pursed lips, fearing that if I opened them any further, my vast lunch would come spilling out like Hudson River overflow. The Second Avenue Deli, in Manhattan's Lower East Side, is not a place for picky eaters, but it does some of the finest Kosher soul food in town. This was my first experience of a proper New York Kosher deli – not the second rate pap purveyors that seem to blight every street corner with their Boar's Head brand 'meat' – and I was suffering. The menu read like a comfort-food lover's gospel, and, not for the first time, I had underestimated the size of New York portions. We'd started with a saucer of perfectly puckering pickles, before moving on to Matzoh ball soup, deep golden and flecked with shimmering fat, a few franks in blankets, a couple of hotdogs and finishing – but I could not even start it – with pastrami on rye sandwich, eight foot high and dangerous. This sumptuous spread fits with most people's views of Jewish cuisine; rich, belly-filling grub that makes up in flavour and warmth what it lacks in delicacy. But the food in question is representative of just one style of Jewish cookery, that of the Ashkenazi Jews. Their roots lie in Russia and Eastern Europe, and the food had to be robust enough to sustain the bitterly cold winters. At the opposite end of the scale is the food of the Sephardi Jews, whose ancestors came from the Iberian Peninsula, and spread to the Mediterranean, Near East and Africa. Sun-drenched, exotic and carefully spiced, the only real similarity between the two cuisines is a varying adherence to Jewish dietary laws.

Claudia Roden writes lyrically on these matters in *The Book of Jewish Food*. But she does point out that, 'There is really no such thing as Jewish food. What is familiar here as Jewish food is totally unknown to the Jews of Egypt, Morocco and India. Local regional food becomes Jewish when it travels with Jews to new homelands.' But although it might be hard to pin down, all kosher food, from whatever region, adheres to certain rules. Kashrut, based upon the Torah (the first five books of the Bible), is the body of Jewish law dealing with food choice and preparation. Kosher describes food that meets these standards, and is not a style of cooking, rather food prepared in accordance with Kashrut. The passages in the Torah are rather brief, and so open to all manner of differing interpretations. But the following rules are set in stone; only animals that 'chew the cud and possess cloven hooves' may be eaten. So pork is forbidden. Lobster and shell-fish are a no-no, as only fish with both 'scales and skin' can be consumed. And frogs, snails and any other '… creeping thing which creepeth upon the earth,' along with any kind of animal or bird blood, are ver-boten. The slaughter of beasts must take place in a specially prescribed, ritual manner (a swift throat slice) to be classed kosher, and drained of any blood.

It's not just the ingredients, but the cooking of food that are governed by a series of religious laws. As no work is to be done on the Sabbath, no fingers lifted, or fires lit, there is a profusion of wonderful pre-pre-pared one-pot dishes like the mighty Ashkenazi cholent – thick with meat, potatoes, barley and beans – or the Sephardi dafina, packed with meat, beans, wheat or rice and hard-boiled eggs. Meat and dairy must never mix, with the strictest followers of Kosher law even having separate knives, boards and areas for the two; Orthodox Jews tend to interpret these laws down to the last letter, while Conservative Jews might be a little less stringent. And the Jews of the Reform Church might even overlook a couple. That's not to say that every person follows them religiously; most of my Jewish friends are a little blasé when it comes to scrimping on bacon and lobster. And even the most devout-seeming rabbi might occasionally slip. A great photographer once told me a story of his youth; some-where on the coast for a synagogue away-day, he and his father sneaked away from the main group to indulge in a little guilty 'lobby'. Just as they were cracking the claws, who should slip in with the very same order but the chief rabbi. But from within these strict confines, a startlingly varied and beautiful cuisine has emerged.

Religious festivals are times where food plays a central role, and these traditions and rituals still run strong. Pesah, or Passover, is the most important of all and sees the symbolic Seder plate divided into karpas (a green vegetable such as parsley or lettuce), representing new growth. It's dipped into salt water, symbolizing the tears of slaves; marror, or bitter herbs, to remind them of the bitterness of life under the yoke; betza, a roasted egg, represents the sacrificial offering of a roasted animal; zeroah, a lamb shank bone, representing the lamb sacrificed by the slaves on the eve of the Exodus. And haroset, a fruit and nut paste recalling the colour of the mortar that Jews used when building the Pyramids for the Pharoahs. As well as matzohs, an unleavened biscuit to remind them of the time the Jews had to flee without having time to let the bread raise. It's a beautifully evocative melding of food and religion, so crucial to the Jewish faith. Respect for the past and hope for the future is paramount, and food is allowed to shoulder some of this vast responsibility. And aside from the dietary laws, one uniting factor is assured; you'll never leave hungry from a Jewish table.

Jerk chicken

Jerk chicken is a mucky-faced, sticky-fingered feast of succulent flesh and charred, wonderfully spiced skin. Eaten all over the Caribbean – and served with a puddle of incendiary hot pepper sauce – it's chicken taken to high art.

It is said to have originated with the Carib-Arawak Indians who once inhabited Jamaica. A captured chicken or pig would be gutted, placed in a deep pit lined with stones and covered with green wood, which, when burned, would add delicious flavour to the meat. But first of all, the meat would be 'jerked' with a sharp object to make holes, which were then stuffed full of herbs and spices. Nowadays, it's a marinade that adds flavour and I like the chicken to sit for as long as possible – for at least twenty four hours – soaking up the atmosphere. Allspice, thyme, cayenne pepper, black pepper, sage, nutmeg, cinnamon, salt, garlic powder and sugar are all mixed together, and then whisked with oil, soy sauce, vinegar, orange juice, and lime juice. A few diced Scotch bonnet peppers add fruity heat. Every Caribbean island has a slightly different version, but you want that contrast between sweet and hot, crispy and succulent. And although I've made some pretty decent versions on the BBQ – and I visit the Notting Hill Carnival each August just for the chicken – nothing comes near the dribbling juice and crispy skin so perfected in the West Indies. Perhaps it has something to do with blazing sun, crystal waters and one too many rum punches. But it never seems to taste quite the same at home.

K for KEBAB

Your first visit to a late-night kebab shop is a bit like a five day trance rave; if you can remember it, you probably weren't there. And even if this momentous event is forever ingrained in your memory, it's unlikely that you ever returned by light of day. Because the doner kebab is a creature of the night, and one best sampled in a shadowy haze. At two o'clock in the morning, it seems like the dinner of your dreams; curvaceous, seductive and happy to sate man's most primeval urge. You marvel at the carver's art and stare, open mouthed, at the roller's dexterity. The way he blends paper-thin slices of spiced meat with delicate fronds of lettuce, and then caresses his whole creation with a soupcon of salsa di pepperoncino. As you stumble out into the street, ready for the stagger home, the first mouthful brings untold gastronomic joy. Fade to the black and cut to the next morning. You peel open your eyes to find yourself playing an extra in Cannibal Holocaust. Chunks of cheap, bloodied flesh – with a fine white fur of congealed grease – lie scattered across the floor, and gory streaks of jugular red splatter the bed sheets. Across the room, the rotten vegetation makes a desperate bid for freedom from its grubby polystyrene tomb. And the searing pain in your gut doesn't bode well for the day ahead. In short, it's the ultimate beer googles food. It might have seemed hot the night before but the next morning will bring the inevitable realisation that you've munched on a dog.

The Doner is a much maligned concoction, and in the majority of cheap cases, quite rightly too. And every time I pass that fatty cone, browning in front of its two bar cooker, I vow that I'll never touch one again. But late at night, when the booze is in control, I relent. 'Extra chili please, mate' I mumble to the 'bab man. He's seen this chili-posturing a million times before, and smiles gently as he ladles on the radioactive gloop, knowing full well I'll regret my actions tomorrow. Of course, the heat of the red syrup totally obliterates any vestige of flavour, but that's the point. It's the perfect convenience food, containing all three food groups – protein, carbohydrate and fibre – wrapped into one easily manageable handful. Part of the fun is leaving an edible trail behind you as you sway down the road. But the doner suffers from bad PR over here, and it's unlikely that we'll ever find it topping the list of the nation's favourite food. The nation's drunkest food perhaps, but nothing of real culinary merit. Which is a shame, as the cheapo doner bears no relevance to it rather more delicious cousin. Properly prepared, it can be a sober joy. The shish is the perfect example. What could be more mouth watering than tender, succulent hunks of lamb, marinated to juicy sweetness, and grilled to pink perfection? And the plethora of Lebanese restaurants that we're blessed with in this country can knock up a mean schwarma, even though the meat comes from the doner lump. But wrapped in soft, warm pitta, spiked with chilies and draped in a tangy mayonnaise, it's a handful of heaven. Even better, they don't require ten pints of cheap lager to increase their appeal.

Kippers

If only the kipper were more user friendly. One of the stars of the British breakfast, this split, salted and smoked herring has some of the finest-tasting, deeply smoky flesh that I know. But two things prevent it from being a regular fixture in my house. First, bones – herring bones seem artfully designed to tickle, scratch and annoy the back of the throat, as well as taking up long term residence in the gaps between my teeth. Worst of all is when they sit, lodged in the soft palate, not doing any harm, but stubbornly refusing to budge despite noisy hawking and spitting. And forget trying to fillet them – it's a case of 'love me, love my bones'. The other drawback is that lingering, fishy whiff given off in their cooking. At first, it's a delightful scent, but it always seems to outstay its welcome. When you're still finding eau de kipper in your curtains after three months, you do think twice before cooking them again.

L for LOBSTER

The most humane way to kill a live lobster, they say, is to drive a sharp skewer between its eyes. For surgeons, psychos and others au fait with advanced brain impalement, this shouldn't prove a problem. But seeing as my experience of this particular skill was limited to an unhealthy diet of gut-drenched, grind-house horror movies, I felt a little apprehensive. After all, the on-screen nutters were armed with the very best of B & Q and I had little more than a sharpened rod. To make matters worse, my two new purchases were beginning to make themselves very much at home in my sink, scuttling about and totally impervious to the bubbling cauldron of boiling water that was soon to become their watery grave.

Thanks to an impromptu, Piccadilly Line retelling of The Great Escape I was feeling pretty murderous by the time I got the buggers back home. After much deliberation, I had chosen two of the handsomest, grey-blue specimens from a fishmonger in Chinatown.

They certainly looked lively, but their claws were bound with elastic bands and I imagined their cardboard box sufficient security for the tube journey home. But I had grossly underestimated the tenacity of these battle armoured beasts. Just as I had crammed myself into a fetid corner of the carriage, the lobsters made their bid for freedom. They burst out of their flimsy prison, and began a frantic scuttle down the aisle. It took an energetic, and highly uncharacteristic, leap to get them back, but by that stage, it was too late. I was fixed with the sort of murderous stares reserved for Eastern European buskers and immediately branded some kind of warped animal abuser. Despite my utterly fraudulent claims that I was a crustacean crusader, and that this tube journey was the first step in their long trip to freedom – a sort of shellfish Free Willy – I was forced to beat a hasty retreat, a full four stops before my intended destination. By the time I got home, I was ready to tear apart the monsters with my bare hands.

But there was something about the way their tiny eyes followed me around the room, swivelling on the end of their stalks, which made me pause. Their initial derring-do had changed into a rather more baleful silence, and I briefly contemplated emancipating them from their imminent demise. Perhaps we could live together in blissful harmony, one man and his lobbies. Luckily, sheer greed shook me from my setimental trance, and I armed myself with the skewer, readying myself like a matador marking his spot. At the last minute, though, I lost my bottle and bundled them into the deep freeze, where the cold is said to send them into a deep sleep. Sixty minutes later, they were certainly slow, but reminded me of Jack Nicholson at the end of *One Flew Over the Cuckoo's Nest*. Still alive, but barely there. And dropping them into the vat of boiling water soon raised them from their slumber. So much so that they kept bashing off the lid with their flailing claws. I weighed down the lid, and took solace in the bottle. Twenty minutes later, and all my guilt was gone. As I fished out the vividly hued beasts – the red pigment in their carapace is released by the heat – I accepted that one must occasionally suffer for one's stomach. Their flesh was firm and beautifully sweet, its richness tempered by a squeeze of lemon and a dollop of home-made mayonnaise.

The reason for this long and rather rambling story is simple; to enjoy lobsters at their very sweetest and most succulent, you either eat them in a trusted restaurant, or buy them live and DIY. Those dried up, wildly over-priced supermarket offerings just give this glorious creature a bad name. You pay a huge price for a sorry scrap of overcooked cotton wool. I far prefer the Scottish lobster to its gargantuan Stateside cousin, as it tastes rather more delicate and subtle. But lobster flesh is wonderfully versatile, and although I'm a purist at heart – grilled with melted butter or boiled with lemon and mayo – it stands up well to the vigorous spicing of all manner of Asian curries. One preparation I cannot stand, though, is Lobster Thermidor. Smothered in a sickly blanket of parmesan and cream, it loses any of its distinctive flavour in a mess of dairy produce. So although the road to spankingly fresh lobster can be paved with trouble and strife, I'd endure a few minutes of tube terror and sweaty guilt to feast on the pure white expanse of their just boiled meat.

Lamb

Around the start of April, cookery columns are filled with the joys of spring lamb. 'What a beautiful, tender texture' they all sigh, while omitting to mention that these wobbly pieces of flesh are utterly devoid of any flavour. If you are unlucky enough to buy early spring lamb – and I do appreciate that some people buy it for its texture rather than taste – you need some desperate measures – marinades and the like – to make it at all palatable. Better to wait a while and try and get hold of a wether or castrated male sheep; a couple of summers frolicking on the fell and they have more flavour in a single fluffy ear than the young, spring impostors could ever dream of. Make sure they're properly hung then roast them like a normal leg of lamb, just pink.

M for MUSHROOMS

The autumn mists, with all their lure of mellow fruitfulness, never held much appeal in my teenage years. The great outdoors was all well and good when the sun was blazing and the swimming pool shimmering, but once the rains set in, the nearest I got to Nature was a flying visit to the Lacock Garden Centre. Come October, though, I pulled on my wellies and strode out into the dewy fields with unrestrained gusto. It wasn't the call of the wild that drew me outdoors. It was far more cerebral than that, because I was on my annual search for magic mushrooms. You could find me most afternoons on hands and knees, brushing aside blades of grass with surgical precision, and searching for those tell-tale nipple peaks. I never found even one, but I was always convinced that an untouched field lay just around the corner. It makes me cringe to think how many truly wonderful wild mushrooms I missed in my myopic quest for altered states, but at the time, mushrooms were for tripping rather than eating.

We show a shocking neglect in this country for the wild mushroom, preferring instead the impotent squelch of the supermarket button monster. Bland, flaccid and utterly devoid of flavour, they just seem to add soggy mediocrity to every dish. In fact, any cultivated mushroom will come off worse in a competition with its wild cousin, although the Chinese and Japanese adore the oyster mushroom as much for its slippery texture as for its peppery bite. We fear the mushroom, afraid that eating the wrong one will lead to a slow and agonizing death. And we share this fungi apathy with only the Dutch and the Arabs, a mis-matched united front against mushrooms if ever I've seen one. Hunting for edible wild mushrooms takes a little learning, but it doesn't require a Fellowship in botanical science. And the finest specimens are so instantly recognisable to even the most amateur taxologist. The Italians, French, Polish and Russians worship this divine group of free-foraged food, with festivals, mass expeditions and jealously-guarded secret spots. They even have government identification booths, so you can be sure of what you're eating. Over here, you'd be lucky to escape the farmer's gun.

The smell of the freshly-plucked mushroom has as much an appeal as its taste; musty, earthy, sweet and slightly sexy. The very essence of a damp autumn's day. They're about subtlety, and a tantalizing whiff, rather than pure, palate-scorching taste. But when out on my foraging trips, I have a strict league of favourites. Best of all, and frustratingly rare (although sometimes more abundant in Scotland) are the Ceps, known in Italy as the porcini (pig) and in this country as the Penny Bun. With their shiny brown cap, and portly, Mr. Pickwick sized stalk, the sight of a few fat ones can bring tears to my eyes. Never, ever wash them (or any mushroom, save the Morel) as they'll absorb water and be ruined. Just wipe them with a barely damp cloth, or brush them with a mushroom brush, slice them lengthways and check for any burrowing worms. Then fry them up with butter and a good handful of chopped garlic and mix them with fresh tagliatelle, or serve them raw, caressed with a squeeze of lemon and a pinch of salt. The fact that they are so seasonal makes them an annual treat, and their elegant, restrained, but very much pronounced mushroominess makes them, for me, the king of mushrooms. They also dry well, adding a more intense forest floor punch to risottos, pastas, stew and broths. Add a few re-hydrated handfuls to the crappy supermarket specials to pep up the taste.

Rather more beautiful but, to my mind, rather less flavoursome, are the chanterelles, memorably described by Dorothy Hartley as 'a tiny fountain spurting gold'. Shaped like little trombones, they materialize through the autumn leaves, artful splashes of vivid egg yolk. Their beauty is so beguiling that when I spot them, I still glance furtively over my shoulder, to ensure that some veteran gold-digger will not beat me to my bounty. Fried gently with a knob of butter and a clove of garlic (garlic and mushrooms are one of the great natural flavour combinations), then mixed into sloppy scrambled eggs on toast, they're as comforting as a warm hug from a dear old great aunt. The morel resembles a particularly wrinkled raisin, with a mass of honey-combed pockets. You might have to give these sweet little nuggets a small wash, to evict any squatting insects and stubborn dirt, but they work wonderfully with chicken, and a creamy chicken pie, studded with black morel, is the very last word in rural luxury.

Puffballs, those vast, white ovals that scatter the autumn land like overturned ball baskets, are abundant and have a strong, pronounced taste. Some say this resembles sweetbreads, and in terms of texture, I'd agree. They lack the offally sweetness of the perfect pancreas, but are wonderful either fried, or stuffed. The field mushroom is often overlooked as a little vulgar and common, but with its pinky white dome and gooey, chocolaty gills (they get more black as they get older) it's the easiest to find, identify and provides a soothing supper, fried with the ubiquitous garlic and piled high on Aga toast. And don't just look at the ground. Growing from the tree trunks and branches, you might be lucky enough to find the Chicken of the Forest, which makes excellent eating with its meaty taste and wonderful texture.

As I must have made clear by now, I'm not the outdoors type. But mushroom hunting gets me off my indolent ass, as it's a form of shopping without the expenditure, the thrill of the chase without the exertion and slaughter. Don't expect, though, to come back with overflowing basket every time. If you could guarantee a glut, the mission would lose some of its charm. You want to relish that heady, giddy sensation when you spot a group of perfect ceps, and if it happened too often, it would become commonplace. The thrill when it does, however, is almost sexual and as much a pure, adrenal kick as bungee jumping. In fact, it must be a sign of my advancing years that the rush is far preferable to the hours of rainbow hued, disjointed hysteria that I used to enjoy courtesy of the magic mushroom. Antonio Carluccio reckons that 'mushrooms are the biggest present that nature could have given to humans'. And as you tuck into a steaming plateful of parsley specked, porcini pasta, lush with flavour and heaven scented, you'd find it pretty hard to disagree.

Margarine

Why?

N for NOUVELLE CUISINE

Nouvelle Cuisine has become, in the three or so decades since its most recent incarnation, a culinary cuss. It's a description that has become synonymous with pretentious, over-priced and underwhelming food, and a movement that most people now view with undisguised disdain. An American wag once defined it as 'I can't believe I paid ninety-six dollars and I'm still hungry', and he had a point. What started out as a genuine revolution of French cuisine quickly became a by-word for over-fussy, flavour-free food. Ask most people for their memories of Nouvelle Cuisine and they'll grimace for a moment – perhaps remembering the price tag at the time – and come up with some half remembered huge white plate, decorated with a miniscule square of bloody lamb, along with a baby vegetable dressed in Sunday best and a few arty squiggles of kiwi coulis. It seemed to be obsessed with appearance over taste, and if you didn't understand this, you were deemed a retarded Philistine. 'Why can't food be art, and the plate its canvas?' asked the braying snobs who got the wrong end of the crystallized sugar stick. Of course food can be art, and the canvas anything you choose, but this wasn't the primary concern of the Nouvelle Cuisine. At its heart, Nouvelle Cuisine was about change. A small group of French chefs and food writers decided that the ancient, dusty classical French cuisine needed a radical change. And for better or for worse, it has transformed the way that we cook and eat in the Western world.

Nouvelle Cuisine was not a concept entirely new to the French. As Alan Davison notes in the *Oxford Companion to Food*, 'the periodic formation of a 'nouvelle cuisine' is characteristic of French cuisine and one of its greatest strengths'. The simplified style of cooking espoused in Vincent La Chapelle's 1733 tome 'Cuisine moderne' was described as a nouvelle cuisine, so the next revolution was somewhat overdue. Some food historians claim that this new philosophy started as early as 1953, in the small kitchens of a Parisian suburban restaurant called Camelia. Here, Jean Delaveyne was steaming his fish and simmering his vegetables briefly in the minimum of liquid way before the manifesto was set out. And the 1964 Tokyo Olympics were important in its formation too, as chefs such as Raymond Olivier began to be inspired by the clean, flavour-led simplicity of Japanese cuisine. Much was learned from this cool, aesthetic style of cookery and presentation. But it was 1973 that saw the manifesto of this nouvelle cuisine published in *Le Nouveau Guide Gault-Millau*. Started 4 years earlier by Henri Gault and Christian Millau, the magazine represented a modern, radical approach to gastronomy and restaurant rating. They felt that traditional French food was in a sorry state, and the hope for the future lay in a young set of supremely gifted chefs, all abuzz with radical ideas. Bold and forthright, these 10 commandments were set out for a new generation of sinning, false-idol worshipping heathen.

1) Thou shalt not overcook the beef, lamb, fish or fowl. Oh, and the veg too.
2) Thou shalt only use the finest, freshest produce.
3) Thou shalt not overburden the menu with a surfeit of dishes. Keep it short and simple.
4) Thou shalt not overuse the fridge – use it, but don't abuse it.
5) But on the other hand, Thou shalt embrace the wonders of new technology, with its sparkling array of blenders, mixers and shiny steel gadgets.
6) Thou shalt go easy on the marinades, and stop hanging game until it rots.
7) Thou should forget about those darned flour-based sauces, the endless rouxs, bechamels and mornays, instead using reductions. No more covering up of shoddy ingredients.
8) Thou shalt watch thy health, eschewing artery clogging, belly-sagging dishes for the more subtle, cerebral delights of light dishes, wonderfully dressed salads and simply cooked vegetables.
9) Thou shalt stop tarting-up second-rate dishes with unnecessary ornaments. Decorate, if you wish, but never smother.
10) Thou should get inventive, coming up with new flavour combinations and learning to think outside of the chocolate box.

As revolutions go, it was particularly un-proletarian. And eminently sensible. But it represented a middle finger up to the crusty old guard. Brilliant young chefs such as Paul Bocusse, Roger Verge, Fredy Giradet (in Switzerland) and the Troisgros brothers embraced this new art, wowing the gastronomic community with their surgeon-like precision, finesse and scientific approach to flavour combinations. The quality and freshness of the raw ingredients was everything, as they could no longer hide inferior produce behind a blanket of heavy sauces. A learned foodie friend remembers going to the Troisgros restaurant in Roanne in 1980, and eating a tiny piece of sautéed foie gras with a minute dash of raspberry vinegar; she'll never forget the rich, sweet and sour combination, and the rest of the fourteen courses were equally brilliant. Portions may have been very small, but they exploded with well thought out flavour. Out went the flour-based sauces and in came a style of cooking, in haute cuisine circles at least – as feather-light as a cauliflower veloute. Searing, steaming, cooking en papillote and grilling took the place of slow stewing, and crisp vegetables, fresh herbs and intensely reduced stocks became popular. This nouvelle cuisine should be a culinary defibrillator, shocking the palate back to life after years of stodge. The great chefs looked at food afresh, and the empirical constraints of the old cuisine were blown away by passion, verve and ingenuity. You could walk away from twenty courses with a spring in your step, rather than a boulder in the tummy, having indulged in a huge array of sparkling flavours. In the hands of the masters, nouvelle cuisine was something very special, if a little over-hyped. But it wasn't a layman's philosophy and although it might have looked effortless, it was anything but. And once it became fashionable across Europe, the standards started to slip and the original manifesto was more or less ignored.

Suddenly, chefs with little more experience than that of peeling potatoes decided that they were masters of this new cuisine. They could charge vast prices for tiny portions. How hard can it be to dribble a bit of coulis on a vast white plate, plump up a sole mousseline and throw a couple of exotic vegetables alongside? Many chefs were simply not good enough at either sourcing or cooking ingredients to pull this philosophy off. But Bocuse could deconstruct a recipe down to two ingredients and both were perfectly cooked. Just throwing a few cubes of seared duck breast and covering it with a red wine and grapefruit reduction doesn't mean the resulting dish will wow the punter. Even if it does have a slice of kiwi on the side. Ironically, it required as much technical skill as the classical French cuisine. Great nouvelle cuisine was erudite and brilliant. The worst was simply retarded. (And as bad ingredients could no longer hide behind the cover of their sauces, it was all the more depressing.) It's little wonder that people came to despise the sight of another vast plate and tiny portion, when so many chefs were utterly clueless.

The early Eighties saw Nouvelle Cuisine at its peak over here. The supermarkets were starting to fill with impossibly glamorous ingredients, such as kiwi fruit, fresh chilies, avocados, baby corn, fresh herbs and spices and small courgettes. And once the movement hit the dinner party circuit, the end was nigh. As Sybil

Kapoor told me, 'Dinner party food at that time was still an opportunity for snobbism. So that if you could serve a chi-chi nouvelle cuisine dish surrounded by tasteless baby vegetables, so much the better'.

Now, the movement is long gone, but its legacy lives on. Intelligent sourcing of ingredients, and sensitive cooking of them, is one thing that remains ingrained. And the link between healthy food and general well-being. It loosened the constraints of classical cooking, allowing the chef an unheard of mental freedom. Once the French destroyed the old barriers, the rest of the world could follow. And did. Alice Waters and Wolfgang Puck were the forces behind Californian cuisine, and modern fusion food – another great concept gone rotten in unskilled hands – was a direct descendant. And its influence can be seen today in the food of chefs like Gordon Ramsay, Marcus Wareing, Heston Blummenthal, Tom Aitkens and Chris Galvin. Nouvelle cuisine might have fallen from its lofty heights, and got grubby on the way down. But at its peak, prepared by some of the world's greatest chefs, it was stunning testimony to a master's art.

N for Nettles

The mottled burn of the stinging nettle is an enduring snapshot of childhood pain. I also remember the clean, green smell that was left behind after we had spent a few minutes thrashing down every nettle in sight. They were the enemy and were destroyed with ruthless intensity. Occasionally, we'd come across the white dead-nettle variety and stop for a moment to suck on its tiny white flower – these have the faintest taste of honey – before continuing, stick in hand, with our daily crusade. I never believed that these noxious plants were edible and not even a Curly Wurly could entice me to put my tongue on its tiny, glassy prickles.

But they are the most easily recognisable of all wild foods, if only for the reason that fear breeds utter familiarity with their spiky form. Mild-tasting, although not as similar to spinach as many make out, nettles are highly nutritious, stuffed with iron, vitamins and natural histamine. Don't bother with macho leaf-grabbing, as they'll get you in the end; just invest in a thick pair of gardening gloves. March is the best time to pick them, when they are tiny young shoots and you can use them whole. Later than that – and forget about nettles after the start of June, as anything later becomes gritty and bitter – just lop off the crown of small leaves at the top. The sting is annihilated during the cooking process, so don't worry about any poisonous residue. Not a jot remains. Although some cooks like to serve it as a boiled vegetable or puree, I find it a little bland. Far better is a good nettle soup, thick with potato, onion, garlic and chicken stock. Serve it with some fresh baked bread and reflect upon the nettle's being a far more delectable friend than it ever was a dangerous enemy.

O for ORGANIC

Despite endless media reports to the contrary, organic food is not the new black. Nor is it a fad, fashion, trend or lifestyle accessory. It doesn't hold the key to eternal youth; it won't increase your sexual staying power; and it can't turn you into Kate Moss. What it is, though, is the single most important movement in farming today (although of course, in the past, before the advent of chemical fertilizers and pesticides all farming was organic.) The organic system of agriculture – one that, wherever possible, avoids the use of artificial chemical fertilizers and pesticides on the land, instead concentrating on developing a healthy, vibrant and fertile soil and growing a mixture of crops – is the salve to decades of ruinous, industrialised intensive farming. Organic farming ensures that animals raised for meat in this country are governed by strict standards of welfare. Organically produced food contains a far lower level of chemical residues. The organic system of agriculture is a sustainable, environmentally friendly one that looks to the future, rather than merely surviving in the present.

And it's not some pie-in-the-sky, abstract hippie notion geared towards a new, green utopia. 'Organic' is a term defined by EU law, and if you want to use it on your food product, you need to hold a licence with an approved certification body. In England, there are a variety of these, but The Soil Association is not only the largest (accounting for 70% of all certified organic products in the UK), but the best. They have some of the most stringent standards in the world, as well as being accessible, pro-active and a powerful pressure group too. The advantages to buying organic produce are equally numerous; organically reared animals will have had, by law, access to fields, comfortable bedding and ample space to move around in comfort. They are allowed to act according to their natural instincts and behavioural patterns, rather than stay cooped up in filthy prisons, and they're not doused in antibiotics, rather allowed to build up their own natural resistances to disease. Illnesses are treated with homeopathic or herbal medicines; only when the animal is in critical danger or discomfort will drugs be administered. The overuse of antibiotics poses a chilling threat to humans too; some factory farmed meat, especially pork, is so drenched in antibiotics that the animals are becoming resistant to certain strains of infection-causing bacteria, and there is now clear evidence that this resistance can be passed on to humans too.

Wildlife is another beneficiary of the organic system, as the lack of pesticides means a greater variety of plants (usually considered to be weeds), insects, birds and mammals. Surveys by the Ministry of Agriculture and the British Trust for Ornithology have shown that organic farming areas have a greater bio-diversity of species than conventional farms. I've seen this for myself at Shedbush Farm in Dorset, where Ian and Denise Bell farm to a Demeter Standard (they farm Bio-Dynamically, which is the very highest standard of organic farming). When they first arrived at the farm seven years ago, there was no bird life at all. Now, after Biodynamic farming has corrected the balance of the soil, the skies teem with kestrels, sparrow, bullfinches, yellow hammers and tawny owls. The wildlife is astonishing too, with badgers, foxes, weasels, moles, voles and shrews, as well as grass-snakes, adders and newts. This is no bucolic myth. With more hedges, wider field margins, herb and clover-rich farmland and a mixed range of crops, wildlife seems to thrive and exists in harmony with the farmed land. Many people are attracted to organic farming by the thought of chemical free food. The organic cynics – who are often closely linked to the vast agri-chemical business – claim that there are negligible benefits to organic; but much of conventional farming uses a vast range of often noxious chemicals, and although these are monitored for so-called 'safe levels', the residues in test samples consistently show amounts far higher than government regulations allow. We also know next to nothing about potential long-term damage caused by the 'cocktail effect' of various chemicals reacting together and increasing toxicity. Organic agriculture is all about maintaining fertile soil for generations to come. A healthy soil gives a better chance of a bounteous crop, as well as giving our descendants something more than a ravaged, dusty patch of impotent land.

Reading the eulogy above, you might think that organic is a flawless system of agriculture, and everything else produces chemically-tainted muck and that any farmer who doesn't adhere to the system is automatically a chemical spewing monster, hell bent on animal cruelty and the rape of the countryside. I don't believe that for a moment. There are thousands of conventional farmers in Britain who treat their animals with the greatest respect, who take pride in the flavour of their produce, and who keep chemical and antibiotic use to the bare minimum. When it comes to meat, the best free-range lamb, beef, pork or chicken is equal to the best organic in terms of taste and texture. In the past few years of being a food columnist, I've been lucky enough to munch my way through some of the country's finest foods. I've spoken to dedicated, flavour-obsessed farmers who either did not have the money, time or inclination to turn organic. Their reputation rests on their meat or produce, and just because it's not organic doesn't make it any worse. Many of them were organic producers in everything but name anyway. Farmers like Donald MacPherson of *Well Hung and Tender* (stunning beef), Chris Frederick of *Label Anglais* (proper chicken), Richard Guy of *The Real Meat Company* and Neil Macdonald of *Cedar Walk Farms* (awesome sausages) prove that you don't have to be certified organic to produce humanely reared, superb quality meat. The same applies to vegetables and fruit too. But when you're sitting in a supermarket, faced with the choice between 'farm fresh' (read 'broiler') and organic, the latter will at least give you a guaranteed standard of quality, albeit at a higher price.

Organic produce is more expensive to produce, and the cost is passed onto the consumer. Whereas intensive, factory farmers can pour on chemicals, fertilizers and antibiotics to make their crop or animal grow unnaturally fast – and quicker to slaughter, and then to market and money – , the organic farmer is faced with a more labour-intensive, slower-growing product. The price reflects this. But just because a tomato or carrot is labelled organic, it doesn't mean that it will necessarily taste any better than its conventional counterpart. In most cases, I believe that there is more depth of flavour, more character, although a walk around the organic section of most supermarkets can be dispiriting. The tomatoes are as wretched and lifeless as their less grand cousins (especially the imported varieties), the carrots are moribund and the lemons lack zing. Although the supermarkets love to wear their green credentials on their puffed-up chests, like strutting peacocks, we shouldn't believe for a moment that they are thinking of much more than the bottom line. People will pay premium prices for organic food, so supermarkets can import cheap, fairly tasteless stock, and make a huge margin. In 2003, sales of organic food in the UK topped thirty one billion pounds for the first time; this is a huge business. But the fact that they are selling any kind of organic produce should not be sneered at; it's frustrating that the quality is not as good as it could be, but the more organic stock that is shifted, the better it is for the organic movement. The main worry is that the first time organic buyer who spends nearly double on a packet of organic tomatoes believing them to taste twice as good because of the price will get home to find a mouthful of watery banality – she'll probably not bother with organic food again. The consumer must realise that he or she is paying extra for a system that is ecologically friendly, and not simply about a better flavour. It's difficult to convince someone with limited funds to spend extra money on something they see as identical to the cheaper version. Sadly, organic food is a luxury that many people cannot afford.

After the catastrophes of BSE and Foot and Mouth (and by the way there has not been a recorded case of BSE in any herd which has been fully organic since before 1985), we are more aware of where our food comes from and how it is produced. We don't need to get all dewy eyed about how perfect the countryside was before the advent of industrial farming. There are as many advantages to the modern world (medicine, technology and education among them) as there were disadvantages to the good ole' days. But the organic system of farming is one to be applauded and supported. Not at the exclusion of other farmers who take painstaking pride in their produce, but as a decent standard of food. The taste, as ever, is crucial, but in this case, it is the way in which it is produced which is paramount. Organic farming offers hope for a fertile future, freedom from (sometimes unknown) chemicals and a respect for the land. Without it, the land will be robbed of its fertility – and by that time it will be far too late to save it.

Olives

One of those foods that I disliked as a child, ignored as a teenager and adored by my early twenties. There was no conscious swing from hate to love – one day I couldn't bear the sight of them, the next I was throwing them into my mouth like peanuts. Their idiosyncratic flavour takes some getting used to, and could certainly be described as an adult taste along the lines of anchovies, oysters and kidney. But while those three are capable of inspiring disgust from their smell or texture, the olive did so by simply existing. The root of this lay in family holidays to Italy, where we'd all gather before lunch and dinner for drinks. I was invariably starving – despite having devoured about five ice creams in the last few hours – and the only form of food available at that moment was a vast bowl of olives. I didn't like them enough to eat – and believe me, I tried – nor did I hate them enough to be happy about not eating them. They just sat there, taunting me with their arrogant unpalatability. And I despised them for it.

Now, I'll eat any kind thrown at me, save the sorry tap-washers that top cheap pizza. Those just taste of salt. But my favourites have to be the tiny, coal-black nicoise, although fat Kalamatas and those wrinkly, almost smoky Roman ones will do me just fine.

P for PIZZA

After about twenty years of slavish devotion to takeaway pizza, my body has finally had enough. And what used to be a hysterically anticipated and much adored staple has become little more than a three day gut ache. It wasn't a gradual process either. One day, I was tucking into a Domino's Pepperoni Passion with undisguised glee, revelling in its concupiscent curds and frolicking amongst its greasy crusts. The next, I could barely swallow a crumb. As falling outs go, this one makes Milton's God and Satan look like a quibble over the bill. Because the delivery pizza used to play a huge part in my culinary life. Not only was it cheap sustenance, yours at the door within thirty minutes (at least if you lived in the city) but it was available well into the night. So if the supermarket seemed like too much of a mission – especially when you were making spectacular inroads into Goldeneye on the Nintendo – Domino's was always there for you, with the Heatwave Guarantee, and a side order of Chicken

Strippers. I knew full well that the ingredients were not exactly wholesome, and I never even dared to look too closely at the pepperoni pieces, for fear of finding an eyelid. But I adored pizza all the same. Now, I literally just can't stomach it. It lodges there like a noxious cannonball refusing to budge.

Of course, the modern American delivery-pizza bears little relation to its crispy based, wood fired descendant. And a mouthful of the real thing is one of the great joys of the culinary world. You want the bite and crunch in the base to contrast with a hot fresh tomato sauce, and the mozzarella to melt in small white puddles across its surface. A properly prepared and cooked crust is everything. A true slice should never droop, rather stand firm when held high in one hand. And while the cheese must stretch and strand like a dairy cobweb, it shouldn't be the dominant topping. Moderation and subtlety are the keys to pizza perfection, along with balance and elegance. And the very finest pizzas use only the very finest ingredients. To compare Pizza Hut 'mozzarella' to the real, creamy buffalo stuff is like comparing a cheapo drip-dry suit to a bespoke three-piece. Quality is all.

Naples is the agreed birthplace of true pizza, although there is evidence that this topped flat disc of baked dough was much enjoyed as long as eight hundred years ago. In Calabria, they had the pitta or petta, in Apulia the pizella or pizzetta and the Romagnans had the slim, crunchy piadina. But in Naples, they elevated this left-overs snack – made from anything remaining in the store cupboard – to pure culinary poetry, and it was from there that Italian emigrants took it over to Uncle Sam.

Arguments still rage as to what exactly constitutes an authentic Neopolitan pizza, and it's an issue taken so seriously that the city has the Associazione Vera Pizza Napoletana, whose members are sworn to upholding statutes that define ingredients, the making of the dough and the precise methods of cooking it. The oven must be wood-fired, and heated to an incendiary four hundred degrees centigrade. This sudden heat rush not only puffs and crisps the base, so that no soggy sections remain, but also ensures that the toppings (especially mozzarella) melt and meld. And wood smoke gives a wonderful tang to the finished product too. A long handled peel or paddle is used to put in and take out the pizza and the whole process is as much an art form as the preparation of true sushi.

The most basic, perhaps, is the pizza all'olio e pomodoro, or marinara. The topping of oil, tomato, garlic and oregano could be stowed on long voyages, so peckish sailors could knock up a pizza on foreign shores. The Margherita was named in honour of Italy's queen a century back, and the white mozzarella, red tomato and green basil represented the tricolour of the national flag. As for the Hawaiian, with its sickly blend of floppy ham and tinned pineapple, all I can say that I hope the inventor – and I'm certain he had not a jot of Italian blood in him – suffers a long and drawn-out death for his sins against good eating.

But despite my new found hatred of delivery pizza, I still remember my first encounters with it fondly. As my housemaster refused to allow them to be delivered to the house at school – he was a gourmand, after all – I had to sneak off to one with a more junk liberal boss. The delay after ordering seemed interminable, but we would hang out of the window waiting for the arrival of the red and blue scooter. We almost assault-ed the poor driver in our haste to get hold of the good-ies, and would wolf down a wagon wheel sized disc in seconds, barely pausing for breath. All that remained was a large grease patch on the bottom of the box. Not all the memories are good though. One pizza gorging experience will stick in my memory for years to come, a culinary snapshot so vividly nauseous that just thinking about it brings bile to my mouth. It certain-ly wasn't the cheapest, or even the lowest quality pizza that I had ever eaten. I would need a book of Biblical proportions to record each and every puke-fest. But it was covered with four inches of bubbling Gorganzola, bluish grey, bubbling wickedly and stink-ing like a tramp's toenail. Just one mouthful of this indescribably pungent mess and my entire body heaved.

I don't deny that my heart now feels a tinge of regret and sadness when I see the Domino's man whiz gaily by without a care in the world. I'll always remember a love that burned brighter than the fiercest pizza oven, a passion that no mere 1.5l bottle of Coca Cola could put out. But we move on, and now I realise that the relationship could never have had a fairytale ending. In the meantime, I'll sate my appetite on the more elegant, poised and adult pizza, a truly worthy successor in my affections.

Pasta

The pasta machine was to the Eighties what the fondue set was to the previous decade. A flashy, slightly exotic piece of kit that was produced once, then left to rot at the back of some dusty cupboard. There were a few deluded cooks who cranked out metre after metre of ridiculously flavoured fresh pasta (garlic tagliatelle anyone?) in the vain belief that fresh pasta was somehow better, less common and more sophisticated than the dried stuff. They probably still believe it now, as they spray the room with orange juice, courtesy of their useless Phillipe Starck juicer. It's like red and white wine – they share a name and a common ingredient, then go their separate ways.

The flavour of the fresh stuff is totally different from the dried. Made with the softest dopio zero (or double zero) flour and fresh, free-range eggs with saffrony yolk, it's divine. And perfect for ravioli, cappelletti, lasagne and cannelloni. Freshly shaved white truffles cry out for fresh tagliatelle, dressed with a soupçon of butter. But avoid the chill-cabinet varieties like the plague, unless you trust your deli. The majority are like sucking starch.

Dry pasta should be chosen with equal care. You want it made with traditional bronze dies (perforated plates for shaping) to give the pasta a rough, porous edge so that the sauce sticks to it. And the words 'pasta di grano duro' are a prerequisite for decent dried pasta. Anyone who eats that brown, wholemeal stuff is probably a hippie and too zonked to notice that it tastes of grit. You should match your pasta to your sauce with precision. Always be aware of surface to volume ratio – short pasta shape and tubes like penne, macaroni, conchiglie (shells) and rigatoni go best with the thick, chunky winter warming sauces like Amatriciana and ragu Bolognese. The more robust the bits in the sauce, the bigger the cup or hollow needed to trap them. Slippery, more delicate sauces like arrabiatta and pesto suit strands and ribbons more, so they remain separate and slippery, perfect for mopping up the juices.

Q for QUICHE

This snivelling, soggy drip of a dish, with its flaky short crust pastry and insipid eggy filling, deserves no mercy. How, I hear you cry, can such an innocuous seeming home-counties staple inspire such hatred? With no trouble at all. It takes two of the finest ingredients known to mankind – the egg and the pig – and violates them most un-naturally. It makes the beautiful mundane, and never fails to disappoint the expectant stomach. In short, it's an affront to good taste and gastronomic sensibility. Real men might have breathed a sigh of relief when they were told that this was something they ought not to eat – but what about the rest of us?

Even its long, inglorious history fails to turn up a single nugget of interest. Did you know that it has its origins in sixteenth-century Lorraine, where it used to be made with bread dough? Or that the word quiche derived from the German word for Kutchen, or cake? More importantly, do you care? I thought not. I've tried to get to the roots of my disdain for this soppy disk, but usually fall asleep without making much progress. Perhaps it was the inevitable disappointment of returning home to the kitchen after a hard morning's play, to find the ghastly quiche smirking at me from the centre of the table. Having dreamed of burgers, pies and thick chunks of sweet ham, it came as an almighty anti-climax. Or was it being forced to choke down the last greasy, quivering scraps of fatty bacon and congealed egg as the rest of the school took to the playing fields? I just don't know. But if it were to be banned tomorrow for sins against the palate, I'd be first in line for the position of Quiche Finder General.

R for RESTAURANTS

There are few things finer than a languorous, exquisitely drawn-out Saturday brunch (although by the time I get up, it's more d'runch than brunch). Wine soaked Friday lunches comes close, but they're still fettered by the dying hours of nine to five life; there's nothing worse than returning to the office half-cut, and spending a hazy afternoon being over-familiar with distant colleagues. And Sunday is too sullied by the thought of impending Monday blues for any real enjoyment. No, Saturday is the day, where the only worry is over the choice of restaurant. But defining the perfect restaurant is an imperfect art, as one man's Ivy is another man's Garfunkles. One second, I feel like an elegant dim sum, the next, a barrel of native oysters, and then a bloody rib of beef. I have no favourite food; what I want depends on my mood, the moon and the time of the day. I do, though, have a few fiercely held convictions when it comes to eating away from home.

On the whole, I like it simple and seasonal. The

occasional foray into the dazzling culinary conjuring of Heston Blummenthal is a fascinating, joyous experience. I love his kitchen chemistry, and his refusal to be bound by the normal rules of the kitchen. You start with a palate cleanser of egg white mixed with green tea. And being Blummenthal, it's frozen in front of your eyes in liquid nitrogen, before being dropped on your plate as a solid lump. Not everything is successful – the dried parsnip flakes served with parsnip milk is the stuff of nightmares, redolent of that sour continental milk. But he has an astonishing skill in the kitchen, and his tasting menu at the Fat Duck is less about sustenance and more about pushing the boundaries of food. If the Trois Gros brothers, and Vergé and all the rest of the nouvelle cuisiners were the modernists, then he's one of the post modernists. Apart from Heston, I like it simple. And the finest simple food is often the hardest to do. Anyone can hide their lack of knowledge and understanding in frothy sauces, gluey reductions and idiotic flavour combinations. But it takes real understanding to produce a perfect omelette aux fines herbes, a consummate tomato sauce or deeply flavoured chicken consommé. It's the same with Indian, Chinese or outer Mongolian (lots of yak milk, I presume); good ingredients, sensibly cooked. That's all. Pretentiousness has no place in a restaurant, especially when carried out by trend obsessed half-wits who wouldn't know a roux from their own ass.

Dress might not seem like an issue, and many believe that you should be smart for dinner. But I'm there to feast, not sashay down a catwalk or lead the first dance. If I pay the bill, I wear what I want. How does a tie and smart pair of shoes add to the enjoyment of a bowl of steamed clams? Do jeans or flip-flops lessen the flavour of a simple Dover Sole? Any restaurant with the decree 'smart casual dress' smacks of an English country house hotel, with their peeling chintz, frozen mussels, and love of garnis. It's not only meaningless – you try and define 'smart casual' – but naff with it. I go to a restaurant to eat, not to fit myself into someone else's idea of acceptable. I might be one of the country's least stylish dressers, but I bathe daily and tip well. The only exceptions are the old clubby classics – if you want to eat there, you pull on the suit.

Service is important, only because when it's seamless, you get want you want, and when it's bad, you forget about the food, however good it is. One of my favourite London restaurants raises service to a fine art. If you arrive early and alone, they'll give you a newspaper so you don't have to twiddle your thumbs uncomfortably. They remember how you like your Bloody Mary, your glass is constantly full without your ever noticing a waiter and a decent break is given between the courses. I don't want to be asked fifteen times if sir is enjoying his onion soup, nor do I want to spend most of dinner trying to make eye contact with a waiter more intent on admiring his own reflection. And please, keep the wine near to me or on the table. Nothing kills a dinner more than a constantly empty glass. Rudeness is also unacceptable, on either side. It's not difficult to say please or thank you when your food arrives. On the other hand, I don't want to be scowled at for asking for another napkin or patronized over the wine list ('Would sir prefer something a little less complex?'). Smiles, but not back-slapping. Expertise, but no smugness. Just let this pig keep his nose to the trough, keep the wine coming, and he'll be happy.

I found out long ago that business and restaurants do not mix, although there's not much to be done about this one. Why ruin a perfectly civilized lunch with stock predictions and cash flow crises? I realise that businessmen are the bread and butter of the restaurant business, but they seem more intent on braying into their mobile phones than enjoying the food. I suppose the fact that less of them drink these days means the volume levels are lower, but it doesn't make them much more bearable. Not all business men are food heathens, but many are. They pile their food down their throat with little regard for pleasure, all the while honking away in their inimitable way. I used to hate the business lunch, purely because I became so self-conscious; I was always starving, but had to wait for a suitable moment before I could get the next mouthful in. These city types should be corralled into a soundproof pen in the corner, and left to fiddle with their handheld, Blackberries and Bluetooth headphones to their hearts' content.

We go to restaurants to relax and enjoy food that we either couldn't, or couldn't be bothered to, cook at home. Eating out is about pleasure, not pretension, and England lacks those decent, mid-level, decently priced places that New York does so well. It's getting better. But ask me to describe my perfect restaurant and I'm stuck. Well, as I said, it all depends on the movement of the tides. Or whatever…

S for SUSHI

It's five am at Tokyo's Tsukiji fish market, and the tuna auction is in full swing. As I tiptoe between the vast carcasses, my hands are pinned firmly to my side. A five foot flash-frozen fish is not exactly the ideal travelling companion on the flight back home, and I get the feeling that tourist or not, one shrug in the wrong direction could land me with a whopper. The mood is one of controlled hysteria, and the atmosphere could be best described as a discordant harmony, as the auctioneer's machine-gun patter mingles with a deafening cacophony of shouts, bells and whistles. I'm amazed that anyone can hear his melodic staccato, let alone understand it, and even our Japanese guide admits that this rapid fire patois is a language of its own. All around me, potential vendors poke, stroke and hew chunks out of the frozen bodies with hooked sticks, looking for colour and fat content; the more fat in the fish, the higher the price. As the auction draws to a close, a tuna traffic jam of electric carts starts building up around the area, wheeling away their bounty to individual stores deep within the vast building. In a few hours' time, the tuna bought here will be whizzed around Tokyo and its suburbs, ready to be sliced into a million pieces of sushi and sashimi. And I spend the rest of the early morning, wandering about the market in awe, mouth agape like the frozen tuna. The fishy smell is negligible, as the produce is so fresh, but I have never seen such a startling array of underwater life. The market sells over four thousand tonnes of seafood per day and if it swims, crawls, jumps, slithers or clings, it's here. A few species seem familiar, but every now and then, my amble is disturbed by some splashing, flapping fish attempting a piscine getaway. The space between the stalls is minute, and it pays to keep your wits about you, as motorized trolleys steam past, impervious to anyone in their way. I pass huge, wriggling vats of slimy dojyo – similar to baby eel – gigantic molluscs by the name of Taira gai, tanks filled with vivid red mullet and snapper and indignant crabs, waving their claws to all and sundry. The shrimps hop about their baskets like crustacean ravers, while the octopuses range in colour from soft pinks to bloody crimson. My eye is caught by an innocuous looking fish, with a rather beautiful tortoiseshell top and creamy white belly. But these little buggers are the famous fugu, or blowfish, and they're so deadly poisonous that only chefs with licences are allowed to prepare them. Sadly, I didn't get the opportunity for some extreme sashimi, but I was told they're a great delicacy, despite being potentially lethal. One thing I was glad to have missed was odd sacs that resembled sunbleached brains. My guide stopped and asked me what I though they were. 'Oh, probably some kind of fish roe', I answered smugly. 'Well, sort of' came the retort. 'Actually, they're shirako, the sperm filled reproductive gland of the male cod'. I moved on swiftly.

An hour into this fishy safari, and my belly was starting to rumble. It can't have been much later than seven, but the sight of all this fantastic fish had sharpened my appetite, and we left the cold neon lights for a slate-grey Tokyo morning. A row of identical wooden huts sat about fifty metres away from the market, and each sold their own speciality, from tempura to ramen noodles. Hungry market workers waited patiently for a free seat, and the line outside our sushi house bore testament to the quality within. After an excruciating, hour long wait – some merry revellers went in just before us, and promptly fell asleep, much to our chagrin – we entered into the warm fug. A bowl of strong, steaming green tea was set down in front of us, and the glistening fish were hauled from a small glass cabinet. Each piece of sushi was made with breathtaking speed and delicacy, then plonked onto the counter. A warm, fluffy piece of omelette came first, pepped up with spring onion. And then it began. Forget everything you've ever tasted before, because this sushi was sublime, in a Busby Berkeley cavalcade, tap-dancing-on-the-taste-buds sort of way. The rice was warm and cashmere soft yet you could still make out every grain on the tip of your tongue. Glittering salmon roe exploded like liquid rubies on the tongue and the mackerel was almost unrecognizable, with its soft, soothing subtle charms, and not the slightest hint of fishiness. O-Toro (the fattiest, and most sought after part of the tuna) sashimi melted like sweet butter in my mouth, pepped up by the merest hint of freshly grated wasabi root (the freshly grated root is a lot less stringent than the nasal, pre-packaged TNT that we have over here) while a slither of pearly flounder was served naked atop its throne of rice, an autumnal dish of staggering beauty. Best of all was the sea urchin, wrapped in a slick blanket of nori seaweed; like concentrated essence of oyster, mixed with iodine, a smattering of sex and what seemed like the crest of a white-flecked wave, it was deep orange in colour, the pure taste of the sea. And I sat, like a grinning Cheshire cat, throwing piece after piece in my dribbling mouth, until I could take no more. This was the benchmark against which I would test all sushi and sashimi; absolute quality, stunningly fresh ingredients and a chef who was a master of the art. Everything else, I feared, would now pale in comparison.

But just because I was in Tokyo didn't mean that every mouthful of sushi and sashimi was so joyous. I arrived, expecting perfection at every corner, and left realizing that Japan, too, had its fair share of culinary rubbish. As ever, good local food meant talking to the locals. And as my Japanese didn't extend beyond 'arragato', it was often a confusing place for the greedy tourist. More than once, I found myself with a mouthful of utter confusion, and the natto (or fermented black soy beans), with its gloopy consistency and smell of well-worn trainers, is not for the easily offended. That one sublime gustatory experience, though, was enough to send me back to England a happy man. You'd be hard pushed to find that sort of

quality over here. Sushi and sashimi, contrary to popular misconception, is not eaten all day and night by
the Japanese. It's just one part of a staggering cuisine,
one where the base, slurping pleasures of a bowl of
ramen noodles sits side by side with the exquisite
poise, elegance and beauty of the kaiseki, or Japanese
formal cuisine. It's a country obsessed by food, so much
so that the majority of television involves cooking of
some kind. Even the bonkers children's shows feature
dancing sushi characters, with an alarming propensi-
ty to break into increasingly intricate numbers.

Hyperbole is often employed when describing the
training of the sushi chef, but it's certainly not something that you'd want Ainsley whipping up on Ready,
Steady Crap. The trainee spends the first couple of
years just cleaning the fish and washing the rice.
Then he must learn to master the perfect cooking of it.
Perfection involves steaming the rice and tossing it in
a dressing made of rice vinegar seasoned with sugar
and salt while a minion stands by, fanning it to cool it
quickly. You want the chewiness and shine so prized
by sushi connoisseurs. There is as much emphasis on
presentation as there is on flavour. While it is possible
to get very decent sushi and sashimi in England, we
also have the dreaded Yo Sushi! and a thousand other
cut-price hell holes. Sushi is the very last thing you
want to eat on a budget. Gorge on warming ramen
noodles, hearty nabemono (hotpot cuisine) or salty
skewers of yakitori, but don't skimp on the sushi. If
you're going to put a piece of raw fish on a loaf of rice,
or serve it in slices, you better be damned sure that
it doesn't taste like the sweepings from the fishmon-
gers' floor.

The supermarkets might have brought these delicacies to a larger market, but in doing so, have cheapened them to the price of a prawn cocktail sandwich. Served freezing cold, with over-starchy, wallpaper paste rice, they're more useful as weapons of mass destruction than a joyful lunchtime feast. One supermarket even went as far as to proclaim 'Our sushi contains no raw fish'. How I used to laugh at this seemingly brainless piece of information; but technically sushi is anything served on, or within, vinegared rice. Raw fish is the most popular, but not the only topping. Other forms include maki-zushi, which is rolled, and chirashi-zushi, which is 'scattered' across vinegared rice. But I still wouldn't go near supermarket sushi.

One thing that I was sorry to miss in Tokyo, much to the relief of my travelling companions, was the famed odori-guri, a combination of the word for 'to dance' and 'to eat'. A lobster or crayfish is cut up while still alive, and artfully reassembled into quivering sashimi. You literally want it to crawl onto your plate, and the flesh is said to tickle the palate, pulsating with soon to be extinguished life. You want fresh, buddy, well how about still breathing? Dinner and dancing will never seem the same again.

T for Tomato

As a child, I used to wander around my grandparents' vast, humid greenhouse, intoxicated by that lush, green smell of ripening tomatoes, throwing the sun-warmed orbs into my greedy little mouth and imagining that I was cutting a swathe through hostile rainforest. The first bite made my lips pucker for a moment, before releasing a sweet flood of unimaginable bliss. And I was spoilt for choice; elongated, dark crimson, knobbly plums that took two bites to finish next to shiny clusters of ballsy cherries – I could fit about four in my mouth at a time – and unbelievably exotic, tiger striped beauties that looked so stunning that I was torn between devouring them, and keeping them alongside my treasured Star Wars figures. My father and sister are also tomato fanatics and we still eat them like apples, with the merest pinch of sea salt and twist of pepper. But had you the misfortune to be brought up on the mass produced atrocity that is the modern supermarket tomato, you might think my passion bizarre in the extreme.

These bland billiard balls are an affront to the noble fruit, and a deeply depressing non-event. They represent the ultimate triumph of appearance over taste, as the supermarkets believe that all we want is a perfectly formed mass of watery nothingness. In fact they don't care as much about taste as they do about unblemished perfection. These rock-hard mediocrities need to travel well, without bruising, so the growers – mainly in Holland, Spain and Belgium – favour a strain of tomato with a tougher skin, which will last longer on the shelf, and survive the journey untarnished. Picking the fruit early also helps to keep their faces pretty on the trip, and they are then artificially ripened with ethylene (the chemical that the tomato gives off when allowed to mature naturally. But any British tomato marked with the British Tomato Growers Association logo is guaranteed free from ethylene and other chemicals). The ever-so-nice red colour is often little more than a scientific sleight of hand. With over seven thousand different varieties available, it seems rather pathetic that we're stuck with the culinary equivalent of the bride of Wildenstein.

Although we plough our way through an estimated four hundred and twenty million tomatoes per year, we haven't always been quite so enamoured of its luscious charms. Brought over to Europe from South America by the globe-trotting Spaniards in the early sixteenth century, it languished unloved for nearly three centuries. Our ancestors thought it toxic – it is a member of the family Solanaceae and related to the deadly nightshade (potatoes and aubergines suffered similar bad press, for the same reason). Cooks gave it a wide berth. John Gerard, in his 1597 *Gerard's Herball*, described it as being of 'ranke and stinking savour' and this view was dominant in Northern Europe until the early nineteenth century. People simply saw it as an ornamental curiosity, with bushy foliage and curious fruit. Typically, it was the Italians and Spanish, at the end of the seventeenth century, who finally appreciated its charms and by the mid-eighteenth, there were over a thousand varieties being cultivated in Mediterranean Europe.

Despite what you may believe, British tomatoes in season – grown with a little love and expertise – are a worthy equal to their Italian and Spanish cousins, and the sheer volume of varieties means that you can choose between the rich, regal purples of the Aunt Ginny, the striped emerald splashes of the Green Zebra or the canary yellow of the Daffodil. Flavours also vary immensely, from lip puckeringly tart Tigrellas, full bodied Flammes, meaty Marmandes and juicy Pendulinas. They're incredibly easy to grow too, and for the past six years, I've grown around ten plants in organic grow bags by the windows. Water, sun, a few bamboos – for the plant to climb – and a little judicious tweaking is all that is needed to produce a glut of full-flavoured beauty. Once they shed their yellow flowers and start growing fruit, I spend hours staring, sniffing and guarding my crop from flies and greedy housemates. Sadly, I've yet to cook a single recipe involving my home-grown tomatoes, as the moment they are ripe, they disappear into my mouth – not even making it to the kitchen. But in terms of flavour, they're every bit as wonderful as the fruits of my youth.

To be fair, not all supermarket tomatoes are bad, and the recent profusion of different varieties is a positive step in the right direction, although they will insist in displaying them in the awful chiller cabinet (by the way, never, ever keep your tomatoes in the fridge, as it sledgehammers any vestige of flavour). The best way to find quality is to trawl your local greengrocer or farmer's market, and ask to try before you buy. In the supermarket, they call this shoplifting, but an altogether more civilized outside world sees this as quite normal.

I have a dream. In my dream I see myself holding aloft a silver cup, to the adoration of a vast watching crowd. But this is no mere England World Cup victory, or effortless reclaiming of the Ashes. No, I've just been crowned Tomato King at the local fruit and vegetable show, and the world is at my feet.

Tabasco

When we were young, Tabasco was used as an amusing weapon rather than an impeccably balanced hot sauce. My sister and I would roam the drawing rooms and kitchens of our youth, carefully concealing its slim-shouldered bottle in our sweaty palms. When adult eyes were turned, we'd shake a few drops over peanuts or salami, sit back and wait for the inevitable explosion. Spying on the huffing and puffing from under a table, we laughed until the tears soaked our shirts. But one day, we decided to go a step further and empty half a bottle in one unsuspecting fella's Bloody Mary. Shaking with barely concealed glee, we watched the fiery concoction approach his mouth. He paused for a moment – and our hearts stopped with him – then took a suitably man-sized gulp. The details of what followed are a little hazy, but I remember silence, a cough, splutter and low, inhuman moan. The usual chit chat suddenly stopped. A strangled gurgle, then he bent and fell to the floor. We scuttled away and ran for our lives, convinced that we faced eternity in some airless jail. How the hell could we know the man had an ulcer? That evening, my father scolded us into a very early bed. But as he admonished us and turned off the lights, I am still convinced I saw a shadow of a smile flit across his lips.

But that sorry little tale didn't put me off Tabasco's specially-aged charms, and I usually travel around with a bottle, in case of bland food emergency. It has a complexity and depth that other chili sauces lack, and I love it as much for its weathered, vinegar kick as for its heat. I like oysters with exactly one drop rained down from above. Any more, and you lose that delicate tang of the sea. I adore that lingering burn of the lips and back of the throat when you overdo your shaking, and it would be my desert island luxury. As one old timer once told me, in the depths of the Louisiana bayou, 'Food without Tabasco is like a crawfish with no claws. It just ain't right.' Couldn't have put it better myself.

U for 'UMBLES

Umbles is not, as you might imagine, a Uriah Heep treatise on humility, nor the title of Gollum's long awaited autobiography. Its real meaning is a whole lot more palatable, because 'umbles is an archaic, but charming, description of the entrails and coarser parts of a deer, which slowly came to mean the innards or offal (the bits that literally fell off a carcass during the butchering process) of any animal. So, 'umble pie was originally a dish made up of the deer organs.

The trouble with 'umbles, innards, entrails, organs and any other term for 'things within' is that they have a major image problem. And I am sure that most of this disgust and disdain goes back to the seventh circle of school dinners' hell. We are born with a blank canvas of a palate and our individual tastes are shaped by the culinary experiences of early youth. So when, at the tender age of six, we're confronted by a lump of gristle-packed animal organ and forced to swallow every last morsel, chances are that we'll spend the rest of our lives avoiding anything close to that nightmarish experience, and when the torture is repeated weekly for five years, feelings of mere disgust turn slowly but surely into hatred. Every school should be made to sit an Offal Quality and Tasting Test, before unleashing yet another generation of offal haters into the world. School liver is a universal symbol of childhood disgust. Everyone has a story and it has become the card-carrying, badge wearing, flag waving cheerleader for horrific memories of school dinners past. Everything about this pallid, curled up piece of flesh was designed to repel; some of my schoolmates with more vivid imaginations used to claim that it was bought cheap from the local hospital, while others were convinced it was stolen from sleeping tramps. Riddled with chewy veins, unknown lumps and possible tumours, putting it into your mouth was like embarking on a twisted culinary assault course. Cut, open gob, insert, chew, grimace, retch, swallow and start again. This sorry specimen was more suited to the science laboratory than the dinner table, and certainly bore no resemblance to the meltingly tender, just pink slices of calf's liver that were served with crispy bacon and silky mashed potato at home. The sick specimens we endured were almost certainly from a raddled old pig or over-the-hill cow. When it comes to eating liver, you have to insist on the best, preferably calf or lamb.

Equally abhorrent were the rubbery lobes that shared the starring role in the steak and kidney pie. Put this dish in the wrong hands, with cheap, chewy pig kidneys and fatty shreds of shoddy meat, and it becomes an inhabitant of the chamber of school food horrors. Even at a young age, you became well versed in the organ's function, purely because kidneys smelt like a public loo. I don't believe that everyone would adore liver and kidney even if they were sourced well and cooked to perfection. But I'm certain that the vast majority of offal haters have refused to try the damned things again, so devastated were they by their enforced early experiences of all things offally.

That's not to say that I breakfast on placenta and eggs, followed by a light lunch of devilled tripe, and chewy chitlins' for dinner. For all my self-consciously macho 'off-road extreme eating' posturing, I'm not an undiscriminating lover of all offal. Brains are an acquired taste, and in any case, the taste is secondary to the creamy texture, and although I can stomach slices fried in lemon, I far prefer them braised, then made into fritters. But I have to confess that I most enjoy ordering brains to eat in the company of fussy eaters, or rampant vegetarians, as the look on their face as I lick up the last lobes adds much to an already pleasurable experience. Tripe, too, can be stomached only in small amounts. There's something about that off-white, honeycombed flap of stomach which brings an involuntary gag reaction. And yes, I have eaten those endless French dishes that chop it into tiny pieces and smother it with sauce and yes, it still tastes like a mix of inner tube and flattened dog. But at a friend's Greek Easter lunch last year, I ate a traditional tripe soup gently flavoured with lemon and thyme and it was a work of rare beauty, deeply meaty yet ethereally light. It was only at the end, after I had slurped down my fourth or fifth bowlful, that the host informed me about their true contents.

It's not often you're faced with lungs to eat, and if you do happen across a pair, chances are it will be in a hearty stew or minced up and filling your service station steak and onion slice (yes, dear reader, all those cheap meat pies, sausages and pates have a secret whack of the less palatable 'umbles. You surely don't think that they would waste prime fillet on a snack that costs little more than a postage stamp). Still, it's not an item that I would leap at on any menu. The same applies to heart; as it's made up almost entirely of muscle, it needs a good spell in a marinade to make it even nearly edible and it benefits from slow cooking too. But chicken hearts grilled yakitori style on a skewer are delicious.

The greatest of all 'umbles is the sweetbread. The term actually covers both the thymus gland and the larger pancreas, though the latter is the largest. There's something about the combination of rich, spongy flesh and a delicate offal flavour that makes it the most sensuous of innards. And they formed part of the greatest meal of my life (at least, in terms of classic French haute cuisine) at Le Grand Vefour restaurant in Paris, the sort of high-church gastronomic shrine that probably served proper coq au vin to Napoleon and Winston Churchill. The sweetbreads arrived in a gleaming copper pan, studded with black truffles and a smidgeon of reduced pan juices. The scent hit the nose first, and the juices started flowing. There were six of us at the table, and we ate these beauties in awed silence, as if a single word spoken would sully the sensation. Just a little crisped on the outside, they were simply sublime, an awesome mixture of texture, taste and exquisite poise. Nothing will ever match this dish, and it was one that reaffirmed my faith in the grand French cuisine.

I don't expect all you offal-phobes to be running for the Michelin guide after reading this, nor even visiting the butcher for a tender slab of calf's liver. But treated properly, and chosen with the greatest care, offal is one of the under-appreciated stars of the gastronomic universe. It might be cheap, and come replete with unpleasant memories of times past, but I would never, ever deem these saintly innards (h)umble'.

V for VEGETARIAN

I really used to believe that vegetarianism was a fundamentally bogus philosophy, and I thought that my red blooded disdain for all things sandal-wearing was a genuinely evangelical calling, a Billy Grahamesque zeal in defence of the meat eater. Ok, I could just about understand those unfortunate wretches who couldn't bear the taste of flesh, as well as those who abstained for religious reasons. But everyone else was a sick joke; we're omnivores, for Christ's sake, top of the food chain, king of the jungle. No cliché was left un-uttered in my ongoing war against the cud-chewers, and barely a day went past where I didn't berate some unfortunate veggie with my stock rant of 'if we didn't eat animals, the cow, pig and chicken would disappear, and by espousing vegetarianism for all, you'd actually manufacture the destruction of an entire species'. God I was a bore. I'm actually surprised that I wasn't ever bopped over the head with a frozen leg of lamb, like the unfortunate husband in Roald Dahl's unexpected tale.

As I have grown older, the vegetarian has gradually become a figure of respect. Not, of course, those faddish drongos who claim that they're vegetarian 'but eat chicken'. Or the fluffy bunny brigade who label themselves 'pescatarians' – or only eat fish, but no meat – as if a salmon or lobster feels less pain in its death throes than an oinky pig or mooey cow. As meat eaters, we have to take responsibility for the animals we consume; in that they should be reared and slaughtered in the most humane way possible. We must never lose sight of where our food came from. But the vegetarian who does not agree with the killing of animals, despite missing the sweet crunch of a bacon sandwich, a plump sausage or juicy burger, is a person of strong moral conviction, and someone to be admired. I am, and always will be a committed carnivore. And still believe that 'vegetarian restaurant' is one of the most depressing phrases in the English language. It's just that I'll defend the veggie now, rather than pour ignorant vitriol on his head.

But whenever I hear the name PETA (or People for The Ethical Treatment of Animals), I start to regress to the feelings of old. Because this organisation is so fundamentally misguided, hypocritical and downright nutty that 'animal lover' is a gross misnomer. I'm happy to admit that not all of its supporters are grinning thugs – just anthropomorphic suckers. And their campaigns against the likes of Kentucky Fried Chicken and Burger King have done much to improve the lot of the broiler chicken and factory farmed cow in America. So far, so laudable. But PETA is an animal rights organisation driven by a hatred of humans.

In fact, most of us are their sworn enemies just for eating meat, drinking milk or wearing leather. As is anyone else who dares disagree with their utopian mission statement that 'animals are not ours to eat, wear, experiment on or use for entertainment'. They see little difference between the twisted animal abuser and the mother who feeds her children meat. 'Feeding kids meat is child abuse' was the slogan for one of their less extreme campaigns.

This is a group which compared the slaughter of livestock to the Holocaust, with an exhibition called 'Holocaust on Your Plate'. In it, they juxtaposed images of emaciated Jews in World War Two concentration camps with starving cows, and showed photographs of human bodies piled next to pig bodies. It aimed to show 'how factory farms mimicked Nazi death camps.', and also compared the death of six million Jews to the demise of six million chickens. This sort of vulgar trash only serves to set back the campaign against factory farming, not promote it. But to Newkirk and PETA, such offensive, demeaning rubbish is worth every penny if it generates publicity. 'We are', she admits, 'complete press sluts'.

For all their moral outrage, they're riddled with hypocrisy. If you'd ventured onto their website a year or so ago, you would have seen a pop-up advert for the Burger King Veggie Whopper. They'll attack the company on the one hand – and for valid reasons too – while grabbing their cash with the other. And then there's the delicious irony of their experiment to see if fish feel pain. PETA-funded scientists inject the little fishies with bee poison and acetic acid, something that seems mighty close to the activities of innocent scientists targeted by these freaks. The true vegetarian course is a noble and peaceful one far removed from the brainless antics of PETA. But for me a life without meat is a life not worth living.

W for
WORCESTERSHIRE
SAUCE

The Worcestershire sauce story seemed at first to bear all the hallmarks of a thrilling colonial romp; ancient recipes, shifty locals, chance discoveries, fame, fortune and lashings of mystery. The tale went, as I believed it, that at Lea Perrins chemist in Worcestershire, a barrel of spiced vinegar was ordered by a customer (you try asking for that at the local Superdrug) who wanted it prepared to an Indian recipe. He never came back, and the brew sat for some years in the cellar. An employee was about to throw it out but decided to have a taste. And that taste turned into a multi-million pound empire. The story was suitably vague, and seemed to say as much about what you used to be able to buy down the chemist as it does about the ingenuity of Anglo-Indian cuisine. I loved the fact that the mysterious vinegar connoisseur never turned up to collect his concoction, as it is hardly the sort of thing that just slips your mind. I imagined him as a monocled mountebank, travelling the chemists and apothecaries of the land, fooling all and sundry with his exotic vine-gar ruse (although I'm not sure if this particular scam was the biggest earner). Maybe he was big in the flavoured-vinegar market, before losing everything to a one armed card sharp in Kentish Town.)Or perhaps he had stumbled on a dark secret between his home and the chemist and was strangled by a thuggee for hire.) Anyway, he never returned, the liquid began to mature and turned into the much loved condiment we know today.

But as usual, the truth is a little less garish, though not entirely mundane. The mysterious vinegar gent was none other than Lord Sandys, an ex-governor of Bengal. And he did return to pick up his order. One day in 1835, he wandered into a chemist owned by John Lea and William Perrins, eager for them to duplicate a recipe he had enjoyed in India. Depending on which account you read, he either brought in the bottle and said 'Copy this, my good man' or had a sheet of paper with the ingredients. Whatever the real story they made up the sauce. Sandys returned and either said 'Now look here, this is a frightful mess' or 'Take half a crown for your services. Bloody good job' (depending on the source you read) and left. The chemists thought nothing more of this strange brew, although they did make up a few of their own. They hated the taste and just left the bottles in the cellar, gathering dust. A few months, a year or many years later, they came back to the bottles and found that the brew had become rather good. They bought the recipe from mi'lord, bottled it up and made their mint. But the sauce still manages to stay shrouded in secrecy, as it has a magic, top secret ingredient that only two people in the world know of. We know about the malt vinegar, spirit vinegar, molasses, sugar, salt, anchovies, tamarind extract, onions and garlic because they're listed on the bottle. The secret ingredient must be hidden in the 'spices' or 'flavourings'. Many brands have tried to replicate this savoury elixir, but to no avail. There is only one Lea and Perrins.

It is a sauce that I couldn't live without and the very definition of umami, the fifth 'taste' so adored by the Chinese and Japanese. Bloody Marys pine in its absence, Shepherds' Pies lack depth, roast beef just cries out for an initial soaking and sausages just aren't the same without a few shakes. Sweet, sour, tangy, savoury, zingy, ballsy, gutsy – hyperbole is the order of the day with this regal condiment. I would go as far as to say it's a backbone of British cuisine, perking up sorry, insipid stocks and adding its 'instant richness' wherever it sheds it murky tears. This is no mere sauce; it's a bloody institution.

White truffle

The thrill of the white truffle is paradoxical. On the one hand, it packs a mighty olfactory punch, a mix of base earthiness, sweet, whispered nothings and a good dollop of pure sex. Yet once the shaved gossamer flakes drift down to cover your risotto, the flavour becomes a shadow of its former smell. This is the point. The white truffle of Alba is exquisitely rare, and almost impossible to cultivate. It is possible to grow some truffles, but none will ever reach the heady heights of the mighty white. Some prefer the Perigord black, but I find the white more alluring, beguiling and silently sexy. You only get a few months to feast on them, from late October to mid-December. And that short seasonality just adds to their appeal. I love the theatricality of its arrival in the restaurant. The way the chef brings the ugly, warty lump to the table for a first sniff. Then it's the twenty minute wait for something to shave it upon. Fresh tagliatelle, creamy risotto, unctuous scrambled eggs. The scales are produced with a flourish, the truffle weighed and the drama unfolds. The smell fills not only your nostrils but your entire being. I close my eyes and wallow in this gastro-porn, juices running and heart-a-flutter. I never want this scent to stop. But budgetary constraints take over, because at a fiver a gram, these fungi ain't cheap. He stops, weighs it again, notes the difference and disappears off to wrap this dirty treasure in tissue once more. The taste is subtle and restrained, a refined cousin to its rather more lascivious pong. Enjoying the truffle is all about that smell, mixed with the mildest of tastes. It's an entire sensory experience. And this is why truffle oil is so base, crass and bullish. It diminishes this beautiful experience into a slug of oil. It misses the point of the truffle and concentrated, the flavour becomes a yobbish brawler, ready to take out any flavour in its path. Used very, very occasionally, it has a place. But too many chefs think that it's clever, smart or extravagant. It's none of these. In fact, it's just plain criminal.

X for XMAS FOOD

October onwards is a particularly depressing time for the food writer, as thoughts inevitably turn to Christmas. How, we ask ourselves, are we going to put a new and thrilling angle on Christmas lunch? And how many more articles on 'twenty ways to stuff a turkey', 'Me and my mince pie' and 'The Great Date Mystery' can the readers take. One of the more enjoyable parts, though, is the annual Christmas taste test. For the past two years, I've spent days holed up in a South London test kitchen, chewing my way through flocks of turkeys, gaggles of geese, entire shoals of smoked salmon – the first few are wonderful, but after the twenty fifth slice, the taste-buds start to tire – and enough bloody Christmas pudding to sink the Belgrano. Actually, my festive lot is far better than that of many food writers; I'm lucky in having an editor who commissions interesting stories – ones that I actually enjoy writing – and despite being rolled out of the test kitchens on a Billy Bunteresque tummy, I rather relish finding the finest tasting tucker. But traditional Christmas food, I'm afraid, just fills me with gloom.

The best bits of the festive season, except for the presents and the opportunity to swig champagne as you brush your teeth, are the supporting roles, the second string of succulent hams, oozing Vacherins, rosy, meltingly tender fillets of beef, meaty chipolatas, buttery Brussels, fresh bread sauce and crumbling Stiltons. The house is awash with glorious snacking opportunities and I wander from fridge to larder in a merry grazing frenzy. But I really don't get the British obsession with turkey. I blame the Victorians. They brought this bland arriviste into popular society, along with those horribly soppy Christmas cards. Our ancestors were far more open minded, feasting and carousing for days on end. Preparations would start towards the end of October (about the same time I begin to worry about Christmas copy), where the slaughtering, curing and pickling of various beasts would begin in earnest. Lavish opulence was the order of the day for the rich and a typical spread would include Neat's tongue in paste coffins, pickled 'umbles, chopped beef or mutton, onions, and other root vegetables and dried fruit, thickened with bread-crumbs and flavoured with wines, herbs and spices – a forerunner of our dreaded Christmas pudding – smoked and glazed boar heads, swans in pastry and the mighty Great Pye. Also known as the Yorkshire Christmas pie, it consisted of a de-boned woodcock, stuffed inside a pheasant, which was pushed into a chicken, and then the chicken into peacock; surround-ed by stuffing, it was wrapped in pastry and baked. All served up, I hope, by comely wenches and washed down with foaming flagons of ale. The Tudors were equally lavish with their Christmas spreads, with roasted peacock covered in gold leaf and sown back into their plumage and feasts that might even include a real life hunt between the first and second courses. Misery guts Cromwell attempted to put a stop to all this (far too pagan and gluttonous for his liking), but after his death, the celebrations returned with a vengeance. Goose, that rich, scented, dark hued slice of heaven, has long been popular too. I'm not sure why so many people fear this blessed bird. It's very easy to cook, as long as you remember to keep it on a rack in the roasting tin (as it gives off so much fat, the bottom gets soggy and flabby if left to swim in it). Sadly, I have scant chance of getting old gander on our Christmas table; even the quietest plea is met with howls of derision. A thousand years of feasting and what are we left with? Turkey. Give me the lark's tongues any day. As I always take on the role of chef on Christmas day, I do try to make this mind-numbingly boring bird more acceptable. A Kelly Bronze or other such specialist, organically-produced turkey at least has a vestige of flavour and a good massage of butter adds succulence. The trick is to load your fork with everything else, add a touch of turkey, soak in gravy and then the whole mouthful is rather good.

But my misgiving about turkey pales into insignificance compared to my utter hatred of Christmas pudding. Even people who like this sullen, lumpen belly buster can only manage it once a year, which says something. The only good bit is digging out the cash, wrapped in greaseproof paper, and my mother has long given up the annual exhortation of 'Just have a little bit for luck'. Brandy butter makes a tiny amount bearable – I literally drown the tarry, noxious filth in it – but I'd really rather just leave it to the freaks who get off on that sort of thing. I always fantasise that upon lighting this woeful orb, it explodes into a thousand sticky fragments, coating the room like a spray of silage. But no, it just burns weakly and fizzles out. I'm not alone in my distaste for pud. Elizabeth David hated it, as much as she hated all Christmas food. She said that she would far rather have an omelette, cold ham and 'a nice bottle of wine' for lunch, followed by a smoked salmon sandwich and a glass of Champagne in bed for dinner than suffer the indignity of turkey and poisonous pudding. I agree. Christmas is a time for feasting, sure, but isn't it about time we started eating something that we actually enjoyed? Next year, I will be dictatorial at the stove and insist on goose, or beef at the least. But my family will say that it isn't Christmas without turkey. And as sure as Father Christmas is fat and merry, we'll be back to that blasted bird.

Y for YAMS

Yam harvest time in the Trobriand Islands, just off Papua New Guinea, is a dangerous place to be a solitary man. Because for a short period, the women of these idyllic islands are allowed to abduct and rape any unfortunate fella who grabs their fancy. The first time I heard about this ancient ritual, it really didn't seem too frightening. You go off for a wander, swim and quiet fag, and on the journey home, are pounced upon by a gaggle of lusty, dusky local maidens. You finish your enforced gang-bang, grab your trousers and wander home with a whistle and a knowing smile. But the problem lies in not being able to choose your assailants. Chances are you'll might end up with a troupe of facially challenged, twenty stone bush pigs. Regardless of their appearance, if you're unable to perform, they'll not only pee all over you, but bite off your eyebrows and eyelashes too. That way, the whole village can laugh at your misfortune. The men actually travel around in groups to see off the lusty ladies. One local boy admitted it was a little scary first time, but if you just closed your eyes, and thought of Papua New Guinea (the islands are part of the country), it wasn't too bad. The ladies never attack any man from their own village, and once the harvest is complete, life goes back to normal. Every year, scores of hopeful sex tourists flock to the island from all over the world in the hope of some free nookie. But the ladies have better taste than to leap upon any fat, sweating Germans, who invariably return home, unspent and with eyebrows intact.

Upon hearing this wonderful tale, the yam went up in my estimation. In the unglamorous world of the tuber, this underground swelling of a vine stem seemed most dowdy of all. The versions we see over here are dull, lumpen and almost entirely tasteless. I realise that it's an important staple of Melanesian cuisine (Papua New Guinea, the Solomon Islands, Fiji and the like), as well as being central to those of Nigeria and other West Africa. They're much loved in the Caribbean islands too. But as Alan Davidson wryly points out, 'No yams constitute a gastronomic excitement; they are just plain, filling food ...' However you cook these buggers up – and you treat them in the same way as potato – they never really taste of too much. (Cooking is usually essential, because in their raw state, some contain a bitter, toxic substance called dioscorine.) You can boil 'em, then mash them with butter. Or roast 'em, fry 'em into yam balls or fritters or use instead of potato as they do in a lot of West Indian cooking; mixed up with fish and spices, then quickly fried, they're not at all bad. And they're decent when thinly sliced, then deep fried like crisps. But if you've ever had to plod your way through a bowl of foo foo, a West African starchy paste, then you'll agree that the yam will never set the taste buds alight.

Many people assume that the yam is the same thing as the sweet potato, but it's actually from the genus Dioscorea, and totally separate. There are literally hundreds of species of yam, mostly natives to the old world from South East Asia and the Pacific Islands, although there is a small group native to South America. They vary massively in shape size and colour, ranging from small, new potato sized lumps to vast, sixty kg torpedoes. Some are elongated and tubular, and some bulbous and grotesque. The skin might be rough or smooth, pale or purple or brown. And the flesh is usually white or yellow but can be pink or purple too. There are six different species in the Tropical Pacific Islands alone, and the Malays have peaked cap yam, elephant's ear yam, snake yam and buffalo thigh yam to name just a few. The ones you're most likely to see in this country are brown, with white flesh, and shaped like a fat salami. They're often cut open to show their quality, and if left too long exposed, the cut surface seals over. They also store well, and were once used on long sea voyages, where they provided much needed protein and starch.

Poultices can be made out of yams and a few can produce arrow and fish poisons too. One species is actually used as a main ingredient of the contraceptive pill. And this link with sex has always been present, as much due to its penis like shape as its apparent contraceptive properties. In fact, in Papua New Guinea, a man's status is judged by his ability to grow ceremonial, long yams – like the local Fruit and Veg show, but swapping beach for manicured lawns, and yams for runner beans. These yam-gardeners endure food and sexual taboos and mutter all manner of rituals to encourage their growth. The best are then prominently displayed in special yam huts, called after ancestral spirits and decorated with woven basket masks or fans, or with wooden masks and plaques. Apart from that, there's little more that can be said about the yam. In most cookbooks, it just says 'boil then treat as the potato'. In culinary terms, it's just a little dull. And however you dress it up, it will still bore for the world. But if you're a man looking for multiple girl-on-girl-on-boy action, well, you know where to go. It's all in celebration of the yam, they say. Sounds like the perfect opportunity for payback.

Z for ZZZZZZZ

There are some foods so irredeemably dull that they barely register in the mouth at all. Too bland to thrill and too insipid to disgust, they hardly justify the effort of picking up a fork to eat them. To describe this sorry group as base sustenance would be to glamorize them beyond recognition, yet they still have a slavish following. United in their ability to induce sensory slumber, they baffle and bore me in equal measure. I've tried hard to get their point, bond with them and chew the fat, but to no avail. As we're at the start of the final chapter, I feel that I can let loose a little and throw caution to the pigs. These dullards must be dealt with, and swiftly too, before they over-run the world in a mire of mediocrity. And if the food fascist – the result of the unholy union of food snob and spoilt brat – must be invoked, then be that as it may. Because these culinary Rohypnols threaten not just the well being of our taste buds, but the very principles of the pleasures of eating.

I'm here to save you from the horrors of cottage

cheese, of polenta, grits, rice crackers and Quorn. These are the sort of foods that you'd cross the Atlantic to avoid, faceless, tasteless rubbish that bludgeons any enjoyment into bored submission. There's something rather smugly middle class about the above collection, as cursory and personal as it is. I'd rank them as white collar culinary crimes, far more heinous than the blue collared excess of the Cuppa Soup, Big Mac and Pot Noodle. The latter are what they are, and offer pleasure in their own, chemical packed way. But the former see themselves as slightly superior, wearing their cultural credentials on their sleeve, without a modicum of taste to back it up.

To be fair, polenta and grits possess no airs or graces – some people who eat polenta, maybe, but grits are blameless in aspiration. Just good 'ole country maize, pure and simple. Both originally hail from the New World, and while the former is a staple – either served warm or cold and cut up – of Northern Italy, the latter is big in the Deep Southern breakfast. Lashings of butter, gravy, Tabasco, tomato sauce, god anything, is added to both to improve upon the flavour, but to no avail. Eating them is like performing a funeral march in your mouth; a relentless plod, plod plod of coarse-ground carbohydrate. Imagine freeze-dried, grated cardboard, mixed with a sticky dollop of gummy paste and you're nearly there. I've seen butter mountains being melted on them grits to improve the flavour but to no avail. Thankfully, the food fashionistas – the sort of brainless fools who deem that rocket is hot, or purple sprouting is in, or truffle oil is clever (it ain't) – have grown tired of

polenta and it has disappeared from day to day life
though not in some regional Italian restaurants. And
grits have never been big over here, and fingers
crossed that it stays that way. Compared to some of
the horrors to come, they're plain innocuous stodge.
But they still remain a decent representation of very,
very boring food.

Then there's cottage cheese, a wet drip of a 'bag
cheese' – it used to be made at home in a cloth bag –
that sets new standards in watery banality. It's not a
cheese, but a distress call. 'If I'm eating this, my life's
in trouble'. I just don't believe anyone could actually
say, 'Tom, I really enjoy the taste of cottage cheese.' If
a mature old Mongomery or Keen's cheddar is the
Henry V of the cheese world, then cottage cheese is
the second understudy for the second spear carrier, a
rank, amateur irrelevance. Even pigs would turn up
their snouts at this muck, and quite rightly too.
Masticate, masticate, masticate, swallow. Repeat as
necessary. Do not enjoy. It's just one stop away from
the food pills so beloved by science fiction writers that
provide all of your dietary needs in one cylindrical hit.
You want to slap it around the chops with a flounder,
flash in its face, even blow it up with banger just to
get a reaction – any sign that it can offer something
more than white curd. But it can't, and millions of
desperate dieters will sit around saying 'Oh it really is
rather good if you get used to it', all the while dream-
ing of steaming hot chocolate, golden, flaky croissants
and rich, wine-spiked stews.

We are descending rapidly, now, into the flavour-
free depths of the meat substitutes, and a few months
back, tofu would have topped the list. But having just

returned from Japan, where tofu is a million miles from the shrink-wrapped mediocrity we have here, I changed my views. There, I feasted on soups packed with silken kinugoshi and ate the firmer momen, deep fried and served with dashi (broth). The textures were exquisite and while I didn't exactly become a convert, I saw why tofu was so highly prized. Quorn, on the other hand, is just plain wrong. Made up of mycoprotein, which comes from the same family as truffles, would you believe – it is pure matter. Even the most jaded 'eat to live' believer would have to admit defeat when asked for a description. A whole lot of substance, with no place to go. I've had more flavour in a suppository, and twice the fun. And then there are rice cakes, those awful ovals that are nibbled on because they're calorie free. These are the Cliff Richard of the food world. Bland, smug (look at me, only one calorie) and ever so slightly sinister.

As the list goes on, my lids are growing heavy and my taste buds turning off, one by one. Food without flavour, dining without pleasure, chewing for survival; all the antithesis of what good eating is about. To simply exist, reproduce and die is no way to live. But to revel in every mouthful, delight in flavour and appreciate the joys of the table – now we're talking.

ACKNOWLEDGEMENTS

I would like to thank the following for their help with this book.

Christina Appleyard
Sara Buys
Ben Elliot
Geordie Greig
Susan Hill
Sybil Kapoor
Andrew Parker Bowles
Camilla Parker Bowles
Rose Prince
Bruce Shand
Clemency Wells
Stanley Wells